Storybook
and
Heavenly Doll Costumes

by
Mary Hoyer

edited by Virginia Ann Heyerdahl

Published by HOBBY HOUSE PRESS, INC.
Cumberland, Maryland 21502

Dedication

This book is dedicated to my daughter, Arlene, for all the help and encouragement she has always given me.

ISBN: 0-87588-320-6

Table Of Contents

Introduction

Mary Hoyer, the originator of the Mary Hoyer Doll and her fabulous wardrobe, has once again put her talents to work in compiling yet another book, *Storybook and Heavenly Doll Costumes*. This book features 29 color illustrations as well as patterns and instructions for 25 different costumes plus accessories such as slips, panties, stockings, shoes and mules — all to fit the 14in (35.6cm) Mary Hoyer Doll.

Created as a companion volume for her first book, *Mary Hoyer and Her Dolls*, it is sure to become an invaluable aid to the doll dressmaker since the patterns also fit, with some slight adjustments, other 14in (35.6cm) slim-bodied dolls popular from the 1940s through the 1960s such as *Sweet Sue, Betsy McCall, Toni, Maggie, Alice, Harriet Hubbard Ayer*, R & B dolls, Madame Alexander dolls and many others.

In 1937 when she conceived the idea of creating a slim-bodied doll for which she would design knit and crochet patterns, the idea of an undressed doll with patterns and instructions was an entirely new innovation in the doll world. Her doll was sculpted by Bernard Lipfert, to her specifications, and manufactured by the Fiberoid Doll Company. It proved successful beyond her dreams. Initially Mary Hoyer designed knit and crochet patterns for her doll

and then branched out into sewing patterns and instructions, eventually designing patterns for her doll for the McCall Pattern Company. In addition she designed a large line of accessories to go with her doll and kits containing patterns, material and complete instructions for the doll dressmaker to complete the garments.

Mary Hoyer and Her Dolls relates the story of Mary Hoyer and her famous doll, utilizing Mrs. Hoyer's own records. It contains 63 projects and patterns for the 14in (35.6cm) and the 18in (45.7cm) dolls as well as 23 projects for children's items and proved so successful that this gifted lady turned her talents to a second volume, this one featuring just patterns for her 14in (35.6cm) doll. Over a three-year period, Mrs. Hoyer brought out a collection of doll costumes which are sure to please the Mary Hoyer Doll enthusiasts. Some of these costumes are entirely new designs while others are slightly revised copies of those used in the Mary Hoyer fashion shows in the 1940s and 1950s, which are detailed in her first book.

Favorite characters from Storyland are portrayed here and come alive as well as stunning beauties representing each of the planets in our solar system. Each costume has been meticulously designed and the doll dressmaker will find sewing a pleasure!

About the Author

Mary Hoyer, the originator of the famous Mary Hoyer Doll, has spent the greater part of her life creating the playthings of which little girls' dreams are made.

She began her career as a fashion designer in the early 1930s designing children's knitwear for several major yarn manufacturers. Her husband, William, formed a publishing company known as "Juvenile Styles" under which name six volumes of patterns for clothing to fit infants and children, all designed by Mary Hoyer, were published.

In 1937 she conceived the idea of creating a slim-bodied doll for which she would design knit and crochet patterns. The Mary Hoyer Doll, sculpted by Bernard Lipfert and manufactured by the Fiberoid Doll Company, was born and proved successful beyond her dreams. Nine volumes of *Mary's Dollies*, containing over 40 patterns and instructions for knit and crochet garments to fit the Mary Hoyer Doll, were published. Mary Hoyer also designed commercial patterns which were published by the McCall Pattern Company. Numerous kits for making additional clothes as well as a myriad of accessories to go with the doll were made available through the Mary Hoyer Doll Manufacturing Company which the Hoyers formed to handle the business.

Upon retirement, this multi-talented lady turned to oil painting for a hobby and has nearly 100 paintings to her credit. Occasionally one of her granddaughters can talk her into sewing a specially designed gown for one of their Mary Hoyer Dolls.

Mary Hoyer is the author of *Mary Hoyer and Her Dolls*, in which she utilized her own records and compiled the fascinating story of the Mary Hoyer Doll. This book proved so successful that Mary put her talents to work once again and has authored *Storyland and Heavenly Doll Costumes*, a book which contains illustrations, patterns and instructions for 25 different costumes plus accessories such as slips, panties, stockings, shoes and mules — all for the 14in (35.6cm) Mary Hoyer Doll.

A resident of Reading, Pennsylvania, for almost all of her life, Mary Hoyer and her husband now reside in Florida. Their daughter, Arlene, operates a women's apparel store at the Mary Hoyer Shop in Reading.

Color Illustration 1. Birthday dress. When the Mary Hoyer doll was 16 years old, she gave a party and invited all of her friends from Fairyland. Wearing her elegant birthday dress, Mary anxiously awaited the arrival of her guests. (See pages 33 and 34 for pattern and instructions.) *Photograph by Clifford Yeich.*

Color Illustration 2. Cinderella. In her breathtakingly beautiful gown, Cinderella was the first to arrive at Mary's party. (See pages 35 and 36 for pattern and instructions.) *Photographs by Clifford Yeich.*

Color Illustration 4. Fairy Godmother. The Fairy Godmother looks beautiful in her yellow satin gown with tiers of net trimmed in black lace. Her bewitching pointed hat and flowing veil add to her charming costume. She is staying close by Cinderella's side to keep her beautiful no matter how late the night becomes. (See pages 42-44 for pattern and instructions.) *Photograph by Clifford Yeich.*

Color Illustration 3. Prince Charming. Elegantly attired in his regal outfit, Prince Charming arrives at Mary's party eagerly looking for Cinderella. (See pages 37-41 for pattern and instructions.) *Photograph by Clifford Yeich.*

11

Color Illustration 5. Heidi. On the way to the party, Heidi filled her little basket with wild flowers for Mary. She looks perky in her plaid cotton dress and cap trimmed in white eyelet embroidery. (See pages 45-47 for pattern and instructions.) *Photograph by Scott Hime.*

Color Illustration 6. Alice in Wonderland. Looking lovely in her Alice blue gown and matching blue shoes, Alice in Wonderland looks as if she has just fallen through the rabbit hole into wonderland. (See pages 48 and 49 for pattern and instructions.) *Photograph by Clifford Yeich.*

Color Illustration 7. Miss Bo-Peep. Unbeknownst to her, Miss Bo-Peep was followed to the party by her two pet sheep. There was nothing to do but take them in with her. (See pages 50 and 51 for pattern and instructions.) *Photograph by Clifford Yeich.*

Color Illustration 8. Red Riding Hood. Carrying a little basket full of goodies for Mary and her guests, Red Riding Hood arrived wearing her red cape and hood. They are both lined in white polished cotton and her dress is also made of white polished cotton. She will certainly be a welcome guest with her basket full of treats. (See pages 52-55 for pattern and instructions.) *Photograph by Clifford Yeich.*

ABOVE: Color Illustration 10. Gretel. Ready to rescue her brother, Hansel, from all the pretty girls, Gretel arrives looking pretty as a picture. She is wearing a full Tyrolean skirt trimmed in white cotton lace and her shoulder straps are trimmed exactly like Hansel's. Her puffed-sleeved white blouse and stockings complete her ensemble. (See pages 59-61 for pattern and instructions.) *Photograph by Clifford Yeich.*

LEFT: Color Illustration 9. Hansel. Wearing short pants with shoulder straps trimmed in attractive braid and a long-sleeved white shirt, Hansel was next to arrive at the party. His knee-length stockings were perfect to complete his outfit. (See pages 56-58 for pattern and instructions.) *Photograph by Clifford Yeich.*

Color Illustration 11. Snow White. "Mirror, Mirror, on the wall, who is the most beautiful doll of all?" The mirror answered: "Snow White." And here she is in her little frock which she wore to do the housework for the Seven Little Dwarfs. Her dress boasts a tight-fitting bodice in lavender, releasing a full skirt in purple. Her puffed sleeves are made in pale yellow and trimmed with a purple band. Snow White is truly beautiful! (See pages 62 and 63 for pattern and instructions.) *Photograph by Clifford Yeich.*

Color Illustration 12. Miss Muffet. With her friend the spider, Miss Muffet arrived at Mary's party looking lovely in her dress and pantaloons of small pink checked gingham. Will Mary's guests welcome the spider, or will Miss Muffet leave the spider outside to play until the party is over? (See pages 64-66 for pattern and instructions.) *Photograph by Clifford Yeich.*

17

Color Illustration 13. Fairy Princess. Out of nowhere appears a beautiful Fairy Princess, wearing a turquoise taffeta gown under nylon net flecked in silver. Silver braid is used for trim and a small bow is tied at her waist with long flowing streamers. A beautiful tiara studded with brilliant stones completes her ensemble. (See pages 67-69 for pattern and instructions.) *Photograph by Clifford Yeich.*

With her magic wand, the Fairy Princess whisks all of the dollies out of Fairyland to the planet Mars where there will be an interplanetary fashion show.

The judges will obviously have a difficult time selecting between all of these exotic and spectacular beauties!

Color Illustration 14. The first contestant to appear is the exotic Miss Mars, wearing a gown made of lightweight sheer fabric woven with gold thread. Her bodice is most unusual with turned-back cape-collar effect and the skirt is full and completely lined. (See pages 70 and 71 for pattern and instructions.) *Photograph by Clifford Yeich.*

Color Illustration 15. Here is Jupiter's darling. Her gown is made of sheer tricot over lightweight satin. A wide tricot ruffle encircles the bottom of her skirt. A narrow ruffle is repeated around her shoulders and tiny handmade rosebuds complete this lovely gown. (See pages 72 and 73 for pattern and instructions.) *Photograph by Scott Hime.*

Color Illustration 16. Miss Saturn is wearing a purple satin gown with white net covering her full circular skirt. Brilliant sequins encircle her short nylon skirt, resembling the rings around the planet Saturn. The sequins are also repeated on the edge of her bodice. (See pages 74-81 for pattern and instructions.) *Photograph by Scott Hime.*

Color Illustration 17. Miss Uranus is wearing a gown with a sleeveless bodice and full to overflowing skirt cascading from unpressed pleats. Her jacket is ivory-colored embossed lace and boasts a circular peplum. A bow in her hair completes Miss Uranus' lovely costume. (See pages 82-84 for pattern and instructions.) *Photograph by Scott Hime.*

Color Illustration 18. From the planet Neptune comes this captivating beauty looking like the goddess of the sea. Miss Neptune's tight-fitting bodice releases a cascade of soft fullness of satin and net. Her net skirt is smocked with small pearls and the top of her bodice is edged in pearls, also. A wide piece of net is gathered on her left shoulder and swept across her hair and over her arm. (See pages 85-91 for pattern and instructions.) *Photograph by Scott Hime.*

23

Color Illustration 19. Miss Pluto comes from the land of frozen seas and constant twilight. The planet Pluto is the farthest planet from the sun. Her gown is made of shimmering blue satin under a white net coat, trimmed in white fur. The fur encircles the bottom of her net coat and is also repeated in the yoke and her wide sleeves. Looking as regal as a queen with her headpiece made of white fur, this beauty queen will surely melt the hearts of everyone. (See pages 92-101 for pattern and instructions.) *Photograph by Scott Hime.*

Color Illustration 20. Miss Mercury looks sweet and demure in her taffeta gown and Juliet cap, just as though she might have stepped out of a Shakespearean play. The gold braid trimming on her gown and cap give her that final touch of elegance. (See pages 102-104 for pattern and instructions.) *Photograph by Scott Hime.*

Color Illustration 21. Representing the brightest "star" in the heavens is Miss Venus. Her gown boasts a snug waistline made of shimmering silver cloth, releasing a full skirt of royal blue chiffon over blue crepe. Attached to her gown is a flowing cape of chiffon edged in silver braid. The ends of the cape are attached to the shoulders forming a cuff for the wide flowing sleeve effect. A silver headband completes Miss Venus' lovely costume. (See pages 105-110 for pattern and instructions.) *Photograph by Clifford Yeich.*

Color Illustration 22. Miss Earth, the last contestant, is a very elegant and sophisticated young lady. Her long tight-fitting bodice is made of woven embroidered gold lamé. The bodice releases a full chiffon skirt in flame, matching the flecks of flame in her bodice. A soft bow of chiffon caresses her left shoulder. The bow is repeated on her right hip. (See pages 111-113 for pattern and instructions.) *Photograph by Scott Hime.*

Color Illustration 23. Ready for cold weather, our elegant beauty is wearing her full-length princess coat of red velvet. The coat boasts a cape collar trimmed in white fur. Her red velvet bonnet is trimmed in matching white fur and to complete her ensemble, she carries a little white fur muff. *Photograph by Scott Hime.*

28

Color Illustration 24. For an evening out, our enchanting miss wears her full-length strapless princess gown made of white skinner satin. The edge of her bodice is trimmed in red velvet to match her coat. Her long white gauntlets complement her lovely gown. *Photograph by Scott Hime.*

Color Illustration 25. Holding her little teddy bear is Mary in her pink flowered peignoir. The yoke is edged in delicate white lace and the lace is repeated around the bottom of her full skirt. The sleeves are full and gathered to a small band to fit her wrist.

Mary's companion looks so pretty in her nightie which is made of the same fabric as the peignoir. The bodice is slightly crossed in front and her full skirt is trimmed in matching lace. The flowers and satin ribbon are the perfect finishing touches. *Photograph by Scott Hime.*

Color Illustration 26. Mary is shown in her Chinese styled pajamas of lightweight flowered satin. Displayed with her are her slips, panties, stockings, shoes and mules. *Photograph by Scott Hime.*

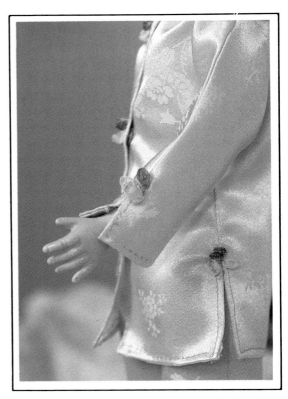

LEFT: Color Illustration 27. Close-up of the pajamas top showing the detail of the rosebuds. *Photograph by Scott Hime.*

BELOW: Color Illustration 28. Close-up of the sleeve and side opening of the pajamas top showing the placement of the rosebuds. *Photograph by Scott Hime.*

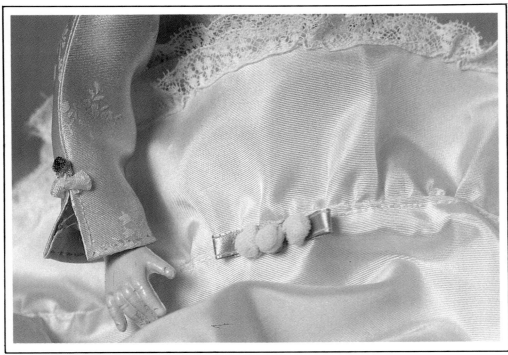

Color Illustration 29. Close-up showing the rosebud used as trim on the pajamas top sleeve and on the slip. *Photograph by Scott Hime.*

Birthday Dress

Illustration 1. Birthday dress. *Photograph by Clifford Yeich.*

Materials:
1/4yd (.23m) lightweight satin or taffeta
1/4yd (.23m) nylon net
1/2yd (.46cm) of 1/4in (.65cm) wide
   ribbon
2½yd (2.28) of 1/2in (1.3cm) wide lace
Satin skirt: 5in (12.7cm) long, 30in
   (76.2cm) wide
Net skirt: 4½in (11.5cm) long, 31in
   (78.7cm) wide
3in (7.6cm) of ribbon for sleeves

Be sure to measure garment on doll as you sew.

BODICE: Place front of net under right side of bodice, sew around neck edge, turn. Sew two darts on wrong side. Starting at neck edge, gather lace on front, tapering to center of bottom as shown on illustration.

BACKS: Place net under bodice, sew around neck edge and back, turn. With right sides facing, sew shoulder seams.

SLEEVES: Sew lace on bottom of net sleeves (stretching net slightly while sewing). About 1/2in (1.3cm) above lace gather to measure 3in (7.6cm) and sew ribbon over gathering. Gather top of sleeves having most fullness at top of sleeve, insert sleeves into armholes. Sew sleeve seams and side seams together.

SATIN SKIRT: Hem bottom of skirt, hem vents at back 2½in (6.4cm) from top.

NET SKIRT: Turn back 1/4in (.65cm) hem and sew on lace (stretching net slightly while sewing). Hem vents at back. Place net skirt on right side of satin and gather both skirts together to fit waistband. Mark center of skirt and center of bodice, sew skirts to bodice having centers meet, turn and topstitch. Sew back of skirts together.

Make small ribbon bow as shown on illustration and sew on snaps. □

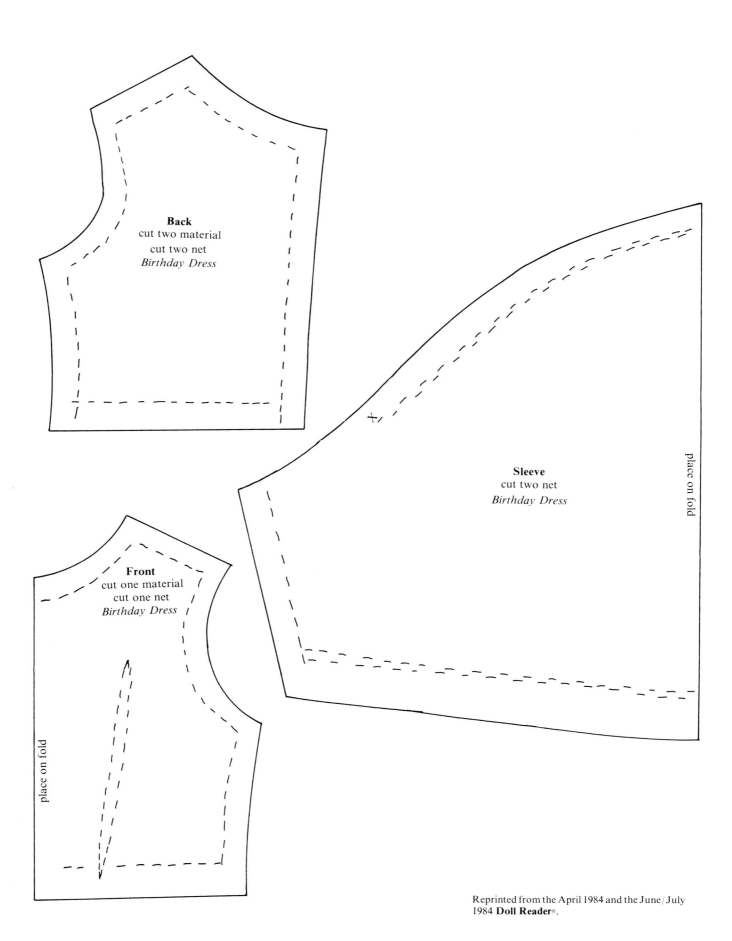

Back
cut two material
cut two net
Birthday Dress

Sleeve
cut two net
Birthday Dress

place on fold

Front
cut one material
cut one net
Birthday Dress

place on fold

Reprinted from the April 1984 and the June/July
1984 **Doll Reader**®.

Cinderella Dress

Materials:

1/4yd (.23m) of 42in (106.6cm) wide lightweight satin or taffeta

1yd (.91m) double width nylon net

Taffeta skirt: 9in (22.9cm) long, 36in (91.4cm) wide

Net skirt: 9½in (24.2cm) long, 38in (96.5cm) wide

Net wide ruffle: 3yd (2.73m) long, 3½in (8.9cm) wide

Narrow ruffle for skirt: 3½yd (3.19m) long, 1¾in (4.5cm) wide

Ruffle for neck and sleeves: 3½yd (3.19m) long, 1⅛in (2.8cm) wide

Organdy slip: 8in (20.3cm) long, 34in (86.4cm) wide

5¾in (14.7cm) of 1/2in (1.3cm) wide elastic

Illustration 2. Cinderella Dress. *Photograph by Clifford Yeich.*

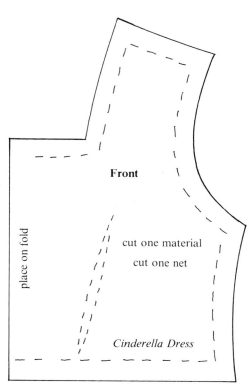

NOTE: Gather all ruffling before sewing on garment. If net is very sheer, net for sleeves may be used double. Be sure to measure garment on doll as you sew.

BODICE: Place front of lining under right side of bodice, sew around neck edge, turn. Sew two darts on wrong side.

BACKS: Place lining under right side of backs, same as front, sew around neck edge and backs, turn. Lay right sides together and sew shoulder seams, turn.

NECK EDGE: Sew gathered net ruffle 1/4in (.65cm) below neck edge.

SLEEVES: Gather bottom of sleeves 1/2in (1.3cm) above ends to measure 2¾in (7.1cm) and sew on sleeve ruffle. Gather top of sleeves between x's, having most fullness at the top of sleeves. Insert into armholes. Sew sleeve seams and underarms.

SKIRT: Hem bottom of skirt. Hem vents at back about 4in (10.2cm) from top.

NET SKIRT: Sew wide ruffle on net skirt, leaving 1/4in (.65cm) below the bottom of net. Now sew narrow ruffle on top of wide ruffle as shown in illustration. Hem vents at back. Mark center of net skirt at top and center of taffeta skirt. Lay net skirt on taffeta and gather two skirts together to measure same as bodice, be sure to have centers meet. With right sides together, sew skirts to bodice, turn and topstitch. Sew back seams of skirts separately.

FINISHING: Sew snaps on bodice.

SLIP: Hem bottom of slip. Now mark center of slip and center of elastic. Gather top of slip to measure about 16in (40.6cm). Sew elastic to top of slip, stretching elastic while you sew, having centers meet. Sew back of slip. □

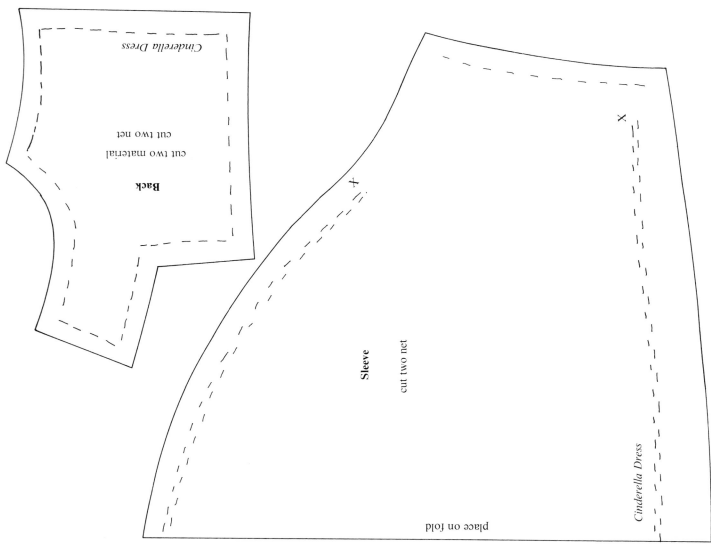

Reprinted from the May 1984 **Doll Reader**®.

Prince Charming Outfit

Materials:

Jacket and cape: 3/4yd (.69m) light-weight brocade or lightweight velvet

Jacket lining: 1/4yd (.23m)

Tights: 1/4yd (.23m) spandex stretch material

Hat: four pieces of lightweight felt

2½yd (2.28m) gold braid

Three tiny buckles for belt and shoes

Be sure to measure garment on doll as you sew.

JACKET: Back: Place lining on right side of bodice and sew around neck edge and bottom, turn to right side.

Right front: Place lining on right side of front, starting at neck edge, sew around neck edge, shoulder piece, front and bottom, turn to right side.

Left front: Place lining on right side of front, sew around front and bottom, turn to right side.

Lay right side of fronts to right side of back, sew shoulder seams.

SLEEVES: Gather top of sleeves between x's, having most fullness at the tops of the sleeve. Now gather bottom part of sleeve between x's to measure 3¾in (9.6cm). With right sides facing, sew top of lower part of sleeve to gathered end of top part of sleeve. Hem bottom of sleeve and sew on braid. Sew braid on gathered part of sleeve. Sew two small darts at notches. Insert sleeves into armholes, having most fullness at the top of the sleeve. Sew sleeve seams and side seams. Sew braid around neck edge and right front.

TIGHTS: With right sides facing, sew fronts together from top to crotch. Make 1/4in (.65cm) hem at top of tights, stretching while sewing. Sew back of tights together and hem bottom of legs. With right sides facing, sew legs together.

CAPE: Lay right side of cape toward you, now fold back wrong side of cape as shown on pattern. Sew ends at neck edge and bottom, turn to right side of cape. Baste bottom of cape starting at fold back at bottom to other end of front. Baste neck edge in same manner. On inside of cape sew braid on fold back of raw edge on both sides. On wrong side of cape, starting at neck edge, sew braid completely around inside of cape and other front. On right side, sew braid around neck edge, leaving ends to tie.

HAT: Crown: Place lining on top of felt piece and sew seam on one side, from top to bottom. Place lining on second piece of felt and sew in same manner. Trim lining on outer edges of seams. Sew these two pieces together and topstitch on each side of seam. Work remaining two pieces in same manner and sew these sections together forming crown. Try on head and adjust to fit. Sew around bottom of crown.

Brim: Place two pieces of felt together and lay lining on top of felt, sew around outer edge only. Trim lining same as for crown. Divide open ends with right sides facing, sew backs together, turn. Place edge of brim to edge of crown (inside of crown facing you), baste together and sew. Turn edge toward inside of crown and top-stitch on right side of crown. Topstitch around outer edge of brim.

FINISHING: Turn brim down on one side and sew on plume. Sew three snaps on jacket. Use braid for belt on jacket. □

Illustration 3. Prince Charming outfit. *Photograph by Clifford Yeich.*

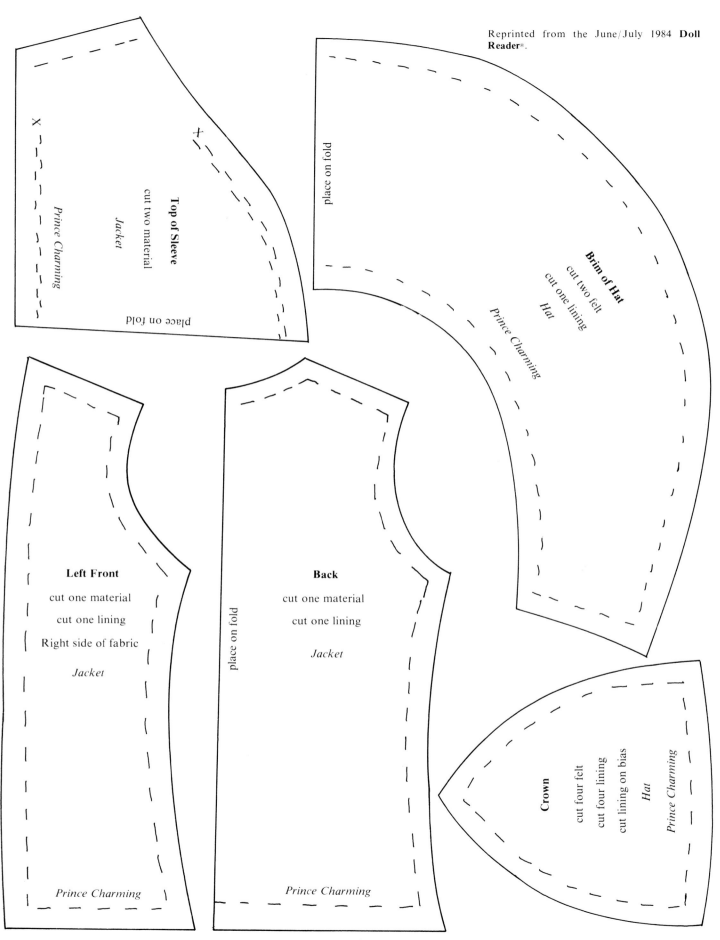

Reprinted from the June/July 1984 **Doll Reader**®.

Top of Sleeve

cut two material

Jacket

Prince Charming

place on fold

place on fold

Brim of Hat

cut two felt

cut one lining

Hat

Prince Charming

Left Front

cut one material

cut one lining

Right side of fabric

Jacket

Prince Charming

Back

cut one material

cut one lining

Jacket

place on fold

Prince Charming

Crown

cut four felt

cut four lining

cut lining on bias

Hat

Prince Charming

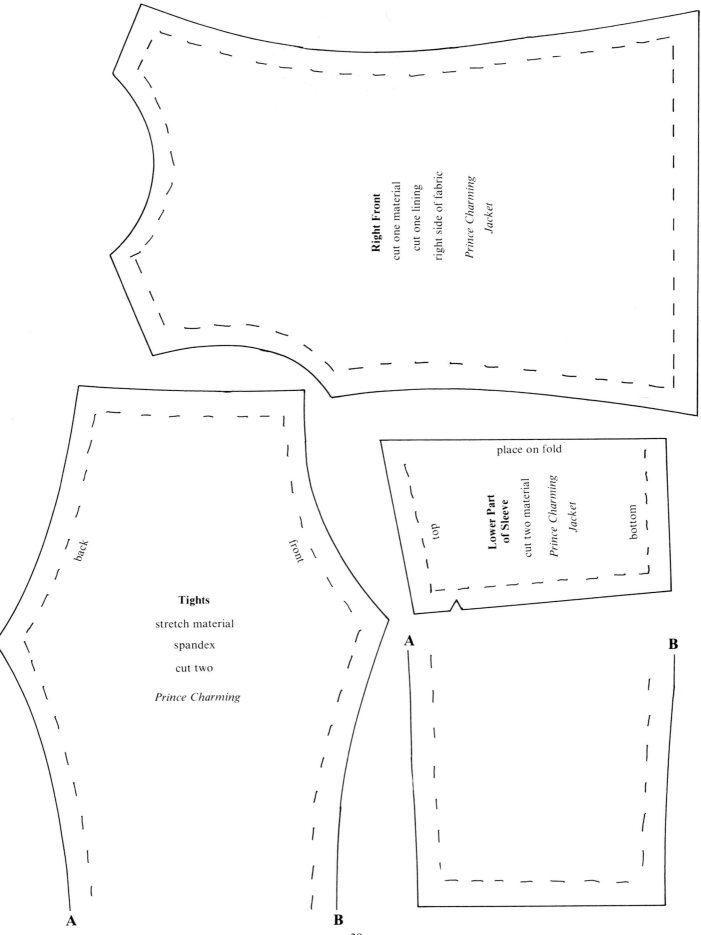

Right Front
cut one material
cut one lining
right side of fabric
Prince Charming
Jacket

place on fold

Lower Part of Sleeve
cut two material
Prince Charming
Jacket

top

bottom

Tights
stretch material
spandex
cut two
Prince Charming

back

front

A

B

A

B

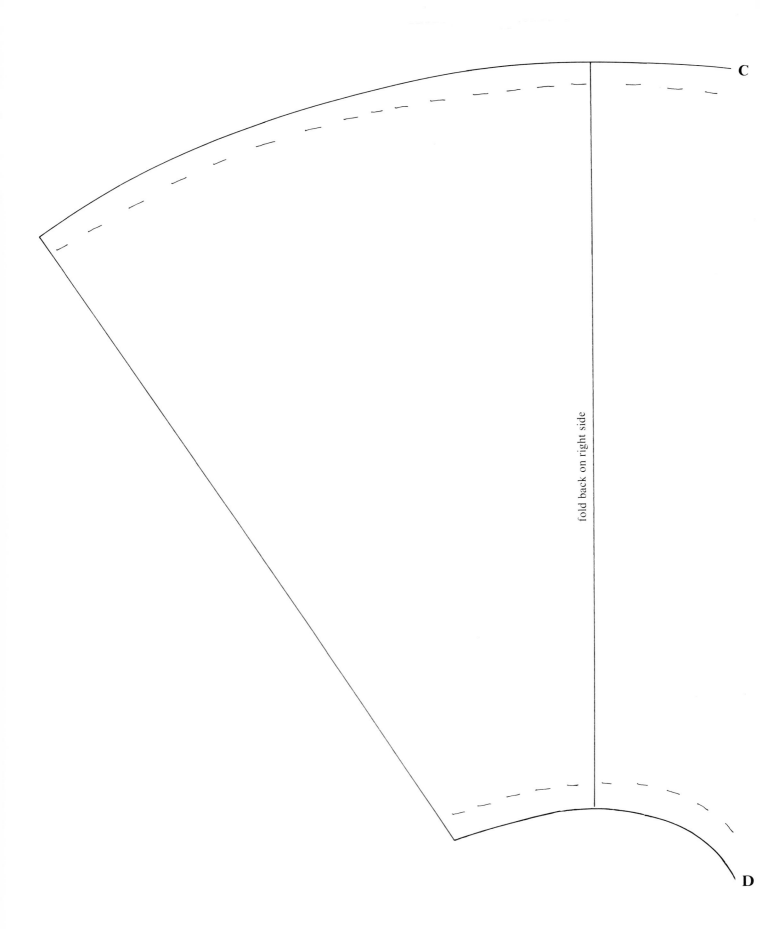

C

fold back on right side

D

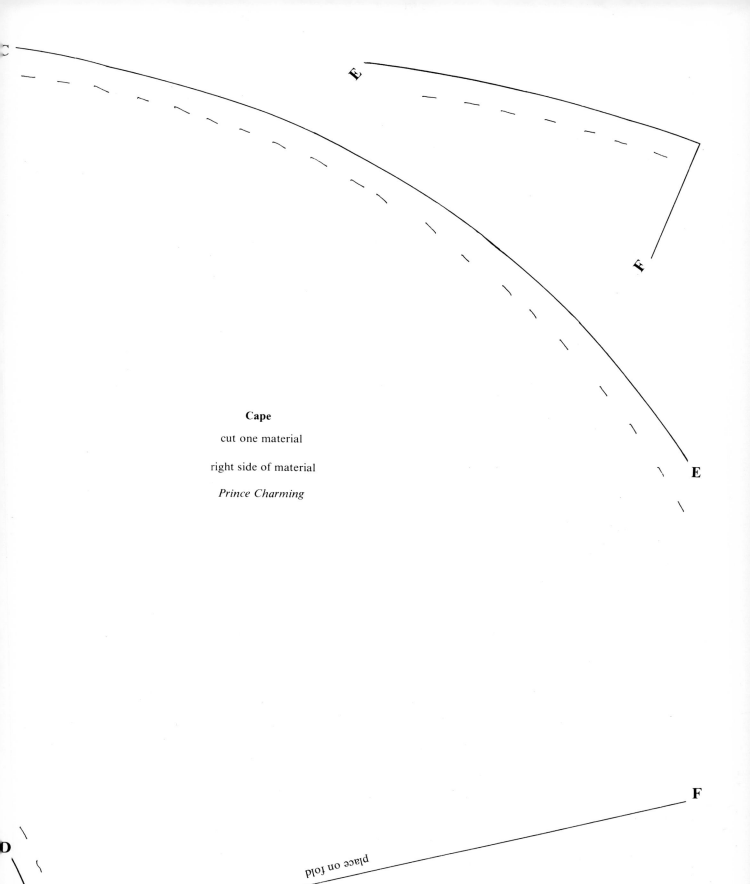

Cape

cut one material

right side of material

Prince Charming

place on fold

Fairy Godmother Outfit

Illustration 4. Fairy Godmother outfit. *Photograph by Clifford Yeich.*

Materials:

Dress and hat: 1/2yd (.46m) satin or taffeta

1yd (.91m) nylon net or tulle

Hat lining: 1/4yd (.23m) buckram

Slip: 1/4yd (.23m) organdy

5½in (14cm) of 3/4in (2cm) wide elastic

3½yd (3.18m) of 1in (2.5cm) wide nylon lace

Taffeta skirt: 8½in (21.6cm) long, 34in (86.4cm) wide

Net skirt, long: 8½in (21.6cm) long, 36in (91.4cm) wide

Net skirt, short: 6½in (16.5cm) long, 39in (99cm) wide

Net veil: 1yd (.91m), 1/2yd (.46m) wide

Slip: 8in (20.3cm) long, 33in (83.8cm) wide

See suggestions before purchasing materials starting to sew.

Be sure to measure garment on doll as you sew.

BODICE: Place front piece of net under wrong side of bodice and sew around neck edge, turn to right side. Place net under wrong side of backs, sew around neck edge and backs, turn. Sew two darts in front of bodice. With right sides facing, sew shoulder seams.

SLEEVES: Gather top of net sleeves between x's, leaving most fullness at top of sleeve. Sew lace on bottom of sleeves and gather bottom of sleeves above lace to measure 2¾in (7.1cm). Insert sleeves into armholes, having most fullness at top of sleeve. Sew sleeve seams and side seams. Gather lace around neck edge.

SKIRTS: Sew lace on bottom of net skirts. Mark center front on all three skirt pieces separately. Hem material skirt and hem a 4in (10.2cm) vent on all three skirts separately. Now lay the shorter net skirt over the longer one, having centers meet. Sew together,

Reprinted from the August/September 1984 **Doll Reader**®.

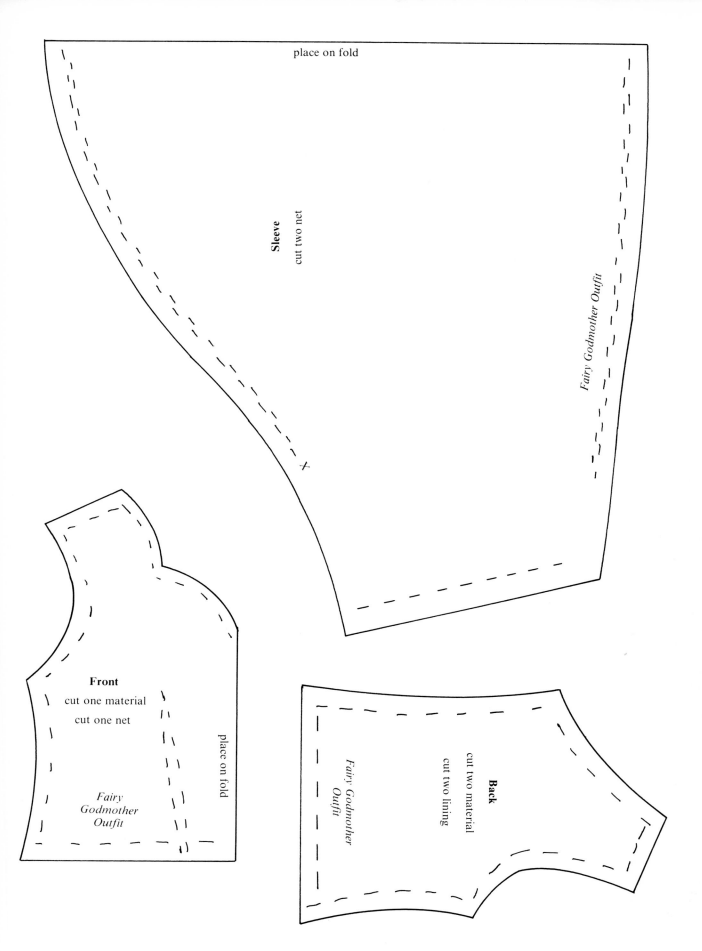

place on fold

Sleeve
cut two net

Fairy Godmother Outfit

Front

cut one material

cut one net

*Fairy
Godmother
Outfit*

place on fold

*Fairy Godmother
Outfit*

Back

cut two material

cut two lining

43

easing the extra inches of the top skirt mostly over backs and sides. Now lay net skirts on right side of material skirt. Gather the three skirts together, easing nets as before. Gather until skirts measure same as for bodice. With right sides facing, sew skirts to bodice, being sure centers of skirts and bodice meet; turn and topstitch. Sew skirt seams together at back, sewing each skirt separately.

HAT: Lay left side of buckram over right edge of piece 1/4in (.65cm) and hand-stitch. Now lay net piece over right side of material and stitch completely around piece, pin or baste in place so net cannot slide, sew seam closely to edges. Now gather widest end of veil to measure same as side of hat piece. Holding net side toward you, sew gathered edge to right side of piece and on right side of edge. Sew sides together, placing veil on inside of piece while sewing, turn to right side. Place this part of hat over buckram and adjust to fit. Now baste ends together and bind bottom of hat with lace. Pin hat on head at sides or sew narrow elastic on sides of hat and place under hair in back.

SLIP: Hem bottom of slip. Gather top of slip to measure about 16in (40.6cm). Mark center of elastic and center of slip. Now sew elastic over gathers, stretch elastic while sewing, being sure to have centers meet. Sew back seam.

SUGGESTIONS: If using taffeta instead of satin, allow 2in (5.1cm) more on all skirt widths. Taffeta is lighter in weight than satin and easier to gather.

VEIL: Tulle or net can be used for sleeves, skirts and veil. Tulle is much lighter in weight than nylon net. Net was used on the doll shown here.

SLIP: Dress may be worn with or without a slip. If slip is desired, use lightweight organdy or some light-weight firm material.

SLEEVES: If sleeves are not tight enough to push up on arms, hand-stitch to fit arms. □

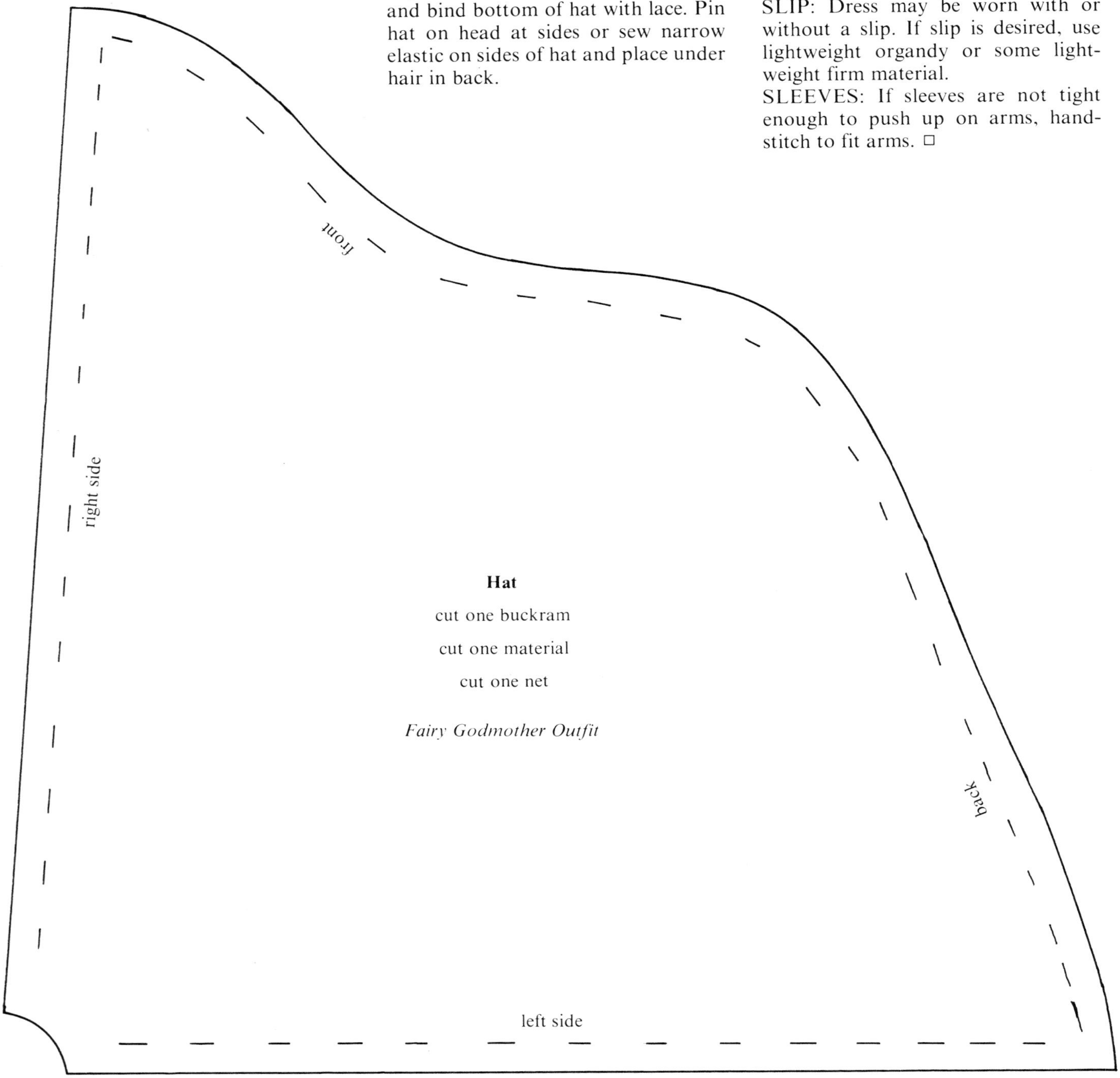

front

right side

Hat

cut one buckram

cut one material

cut one net

Fairy Godmother Outfit

back

left side

Illustration 5. Heidi outfit.
Photograph by Scott Hime.

Heidi Outfit

Material:

1/2yd (.46m) plaid cotton

Lining—bodice: 10in (25.4cm) long, 10in (25.4cm) wide organdy

1/4yd (.23m) eyelet embroidery

Eyelet trim—bottom of skirt, yoke and cap: 1⅞yd (1.68m) long, 1¼in (3.2cm) wide; panties: 1/2yd (.46m) long, 3/4in (2cm) wide

Ribbon: 3/4yd (.69m) long, 1/4in (.65cm) wide

Skirt: 4½in (11.5cm) long, 29in (73.7cm) wide

Sleeve bands: 3⅛in (8cm) long, 1⅛in (2.8cm) wide

Stockings: 1/4yd (.23m) spandex stretch material

See suggestions at end of instructions before purchasing fabric.

Be sure to measure garment on doll as you sew.

BODICE: Front: Place lining on right side of front and sew around neck edge, turn to right side. Sew two darts as shown on pattern. BODICE: Backs: Placing lining on right side of back and sew around neck edge and back, turn to right side. With right sides facing, sew shoulder seam.

SLEEVES: Gather top of sleeve between x's. Now gather bottom of sleeve to measure 3in (7.6cm). With right sides facing, sew band over gathers on bottom of sleeve. Turn band under and topstitch. Insert sleeve into armhole, having most gathers at top of sleeve. Sew sleeve seams and side seams.

SKIRT: Gather eyelet trim and lay right sides on right side of skirt and sew gathered trim about 1/4in (.65cm) above raw edges. Turn to right side and topstitch. Mark center of skirt at top and center of bodice. Hem vents at back and gather top of skirt to fit bodice. With right sides facing, sew skirt to bodice, having centers meet. Turn to right side and topstitch.

YOKE: Baste piece of yoke in place at neck edge at front. Now stitch around entire neck edge. Gather center of yoke as shown in illustration.

Reprinted from the February/March 1988 **Doll Reader**.

CAP: On plaid piece of cap at center back, sew to sides, to form cap. Turn edges of cap about 1/4in (.65cm) across front and back to wrong side and baste. Work eyelet lining in same manner as plaid piece. Mark center front. Measure eyelet trim 14in (35.6cm) long and fold in half, mark center. Measure 2½in (6.4cm) from ends and taper ends to about 3/4in (2cm). Gather trim to measure same as front of cap. Now sew on wrong side of lining, having centers meet and turn ends under so raw edge will not show on either side of trim. Now insert wrong side of lining on inside of plaid piece. Pin or baste in place and sew around entire cap.

RIBBON: Cut piece of ribbon in half and make tiny bows on each side of cap, leaving ends to tie.

PANTIES: With right sides facing, sew fronts together (from top to crotch). Hem vents at back and across top. Cut trim in half and gather each piece to fit pantie legs. Lay right side of trim on right side of leg and sew trim about 1/4in (.65cm) above raw edges, turn to right side and topstitch. Work over leg in same manner. Sew back together from notch to crotch. Fold in half so centers meet and with right sides facing, sew crotch together. Sew on small snap.

STOCKINGS: Fold piece in half lengthwise and sew seam on raw edges, stretching slightly while sewing. When on leg, stocking will stretch to full length.

Sew two snaps on bodice.

SUGGESTIONS: If you cannot obtain eyelet trim without binding, the binding can be ripped off. Then press the trim and gather it. Or less yardage can be purchased than the amount given in the instructions and used with binding on gathered trim. All the trim used on the costume shown in the illustration was without binding. The binding must be taken off when cutting the yoke. □

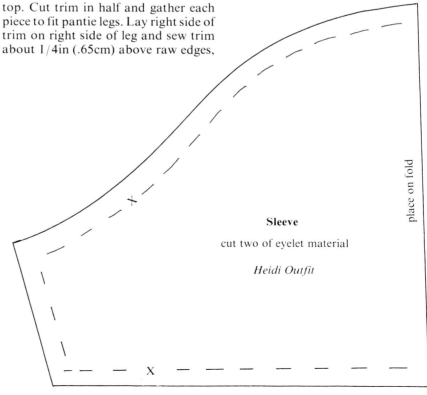

Sleeve

cut two of eyelet material

Heidi Outfit

place on fold

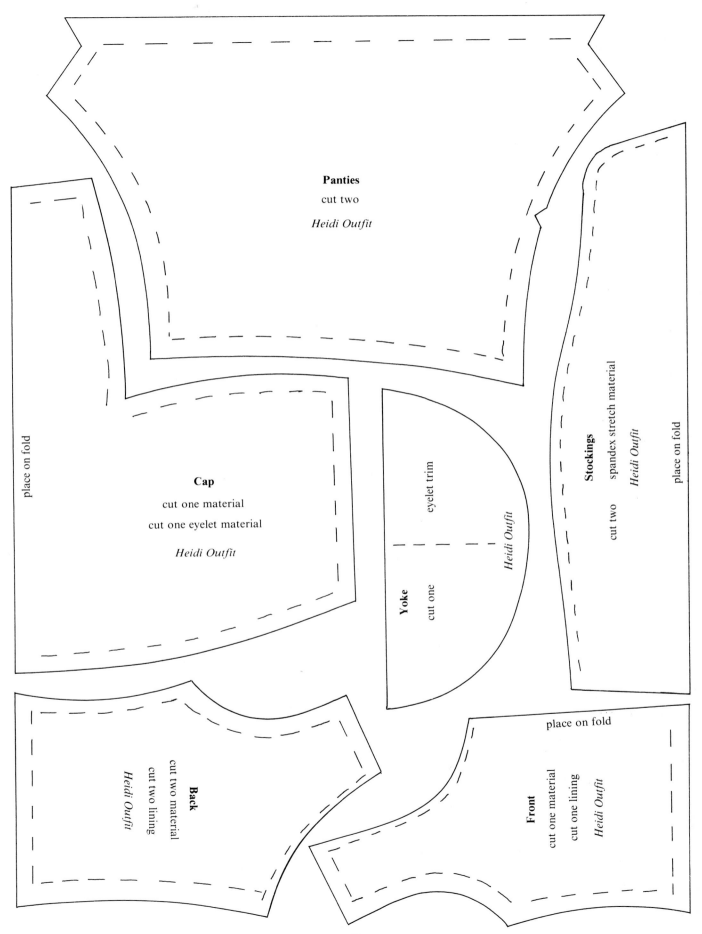

Panties

cut two

Heidi Outfit

place on fold

Cap

cut one material

cut one eyelet material

Heidi Outfit

eyelet trim

Yoke

cut one

Heidi Outfit

Stockings

spandex stretch material

Heidi Outfit

cut two

place on fold

place on fold

Front

cut one material

cut one lining

Heidi Outfit

Back

cut two material

cut two lining

Heidi Outfit

Alice in Wonderland Outfit

Illustration 6. Alice in Wonderland outfit. *Photograph by Clifford Yeich.*

Materials:
Dress: 1/4yd (.23m) "Alice blue" cotton
Pinafore: 1/4yd (.23m) sheer fabric
Skirt: 5¼in (13.4cm) long, 30in (76.2cm) wide
Sleeve bands: 3in (7.6cm) long, 1in (2.5cm) wide
Pinafore: 4¼in (10.9cm) long, 15in (38.1cm) wide
Tie: 24in (61cm) long, 1¾in (4.5cm) wide
1¼yd (1.14m) of 3/4in (2cm) wide lace
Stockings: 1/4yd (.23m) spandex stretch material
Be sure to measure garment on doll as you sew.
BODICE: Place front of lining on right side of bodice and sew around neck edge, turn. Sew two darts in front.
BACKS: Place lining on right side of backs and sew around neck edge and backs, turn. With right sides facing, lay backs on front and sew shoulder seams.
SLEEVES: Gather bottom of sleeves to measure 3in (7.6cm). Gather top of sleeves between x's, having most fullness at top of sleeve. Sew sleeve bands to bottom of sleeve, having raw edges meet. Turn to wrong side, fold raw edges under and topstitch.
SKIRT: Hem bottom of skirt. Sew vents at back. Gather top of skirt to measure same as waist. Measure center of skirt and center of bodice. With right sides facing, sew skirt to bodice, turn and topstitch. Hem back of skirt.
PINAFORE: Hem ends of skirt. Now turn under 1/4in (.65cm) for hem and gather on lace. Gather top piece to measure 4¼in (10.9cm).

SHOULDER STRAPS: Fold piece in half lengthwise and press. Now open piece and gather lace on inside of edge, having lace with most fullness at center of piece. Fasten cord or narrow ribbon on one end on inside of piece. Cut ribbon 1in (2.5cm) longer than piece. Fold piece over lace and baste to other side. Be sure not to baste ribbon. Now sew and turn to right side by pulling ribbon through piece; press.

TIE: Fold lengthwise and press 1/4in (.65cm) in on inside of tie on both edges. Fold piece in half lengthwise and press. Mark center of tie and center of pinafore and on folded edge, topstitch band to pinafore. Baste shoulder straps to center of band inside of folds, having points meet. Baste ends of backs after measuring on doll. Topstitch upper edge of tie including shoulder straps.

STOCKINGS: Fold piece in half lengthwise and sew seam on raw edges (close to edge) and stretch slightly while sewing. When putting stocking on leg, stretch stocking full length of leg. □

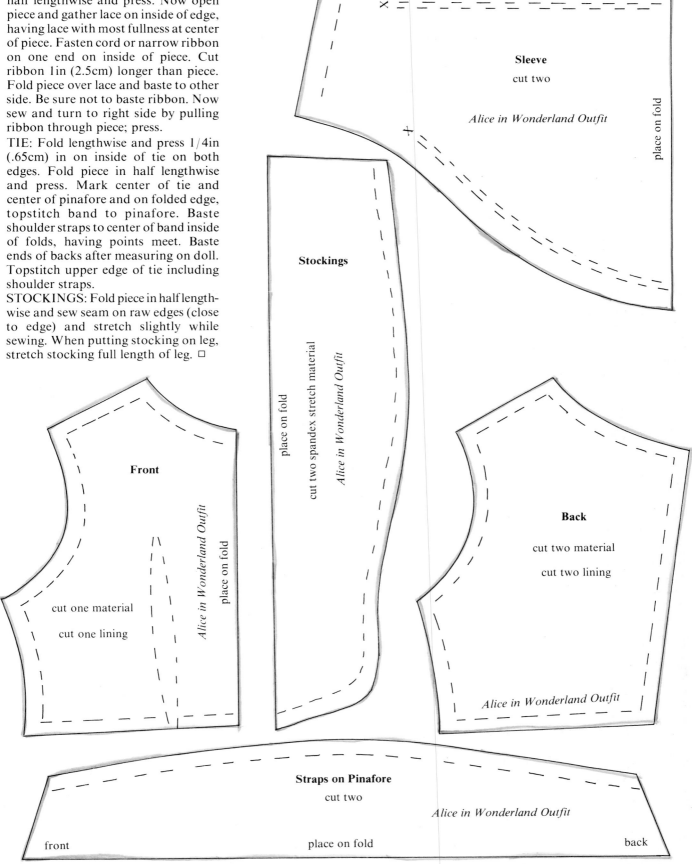

Sleeve

cut two

Alice in Wonderland Outfit

place on fold

Stockings

place on fold

cut two spandex stretch material

Alice in Wonderland Outfit

Front

cut one material

cut one lining

Alice in Wonderland Outfit

place on fold

Back

cut two material

cut two lining

Alice in Wonderland Outfit

Straps on Pinafore

cut two

Alice in Wonderland Outfit

front

place on fold

back

Reprinted from the October 1984 **Doll Reader**®.

Miss Bo-Peep Outfit

Materials:

Skirt and bodice: 1/4yd (.23m) cotton fabric, main color

Peplum and sleeve: 1/4yd (.23m) contrasting material

Lining for peplum and slip: 1/2yd (.46m)

1¾yd (1.60m) eyelet embroidery trim

Skirt: 9in (22.9cm) long, 34in (86.4cm) wide

Slip: 8½in (21.6cm) long, 33in (83.8cm) wide

6in (15.2cm) of 1/2in (1.3cm) wide elastic

Sleeve bands: 3in (7.6cm) long, 1in (2.5cm) wide

Illustration 7. Miss Bo-Peep outfit. *Photograph by Clifford Yeich.*

Be sure to measure garment on doll as you sew.

BODICE: Front: Place lining on right side of bodice and sew around neck edge, turn to right side. Sew two darts in front.

BACKS: Place lining on right side of backs and sew around neck edge and backs, turn. With right sides facing, sew shoulder seams.

SLEEVES: Gather top of sleeves between x's, having most fullness at top of sleeve. Gather bottom of sleeves to measure 3in (7.6cm).

SLEEVE BANDS: With right sides facing, sew band over gathers at bottom of sleeve. Turn band under and top-stitch. Insert sleeves into armholes and sew sleeve seams and side seams.

SKIRT: Hem bottom of skirt and hem vents at back about 4½in (11.5cm) from top of skirt.

PEPLUM: Gather eyelet trim on right side of peplum, with right sides facing. Lay lining of peplum over right side of peplum (be sure to have trim on inside of pieces). Pin or baste in place and sew together around sides and bottom. Turn to right side and sew across top of piece and topstitch. Work second piece in same manner. Mark center of skirt and lay both peplum pieces on skirt about 1/2in (1.3cm) apart from center of skirt and top. Sew piece to skirt. Now gather skirt to measure same as bodice. Mark center of bodice and sew skirt to bodice with right sides facing, having centers meet. Turn and top-stitch. Hem back of skirt. Sew two snaps on bodice.

SLIP: Hem bottom of slip. Mark center of slip and center of elastic. Gather top of slip to measure about 16in (40.6cm) wide. Gather slip with elastic, stretching elastic as you sew, having centers meet. Sew back of slip. □

Reprinted from the November 1984 **Doll Reader**.

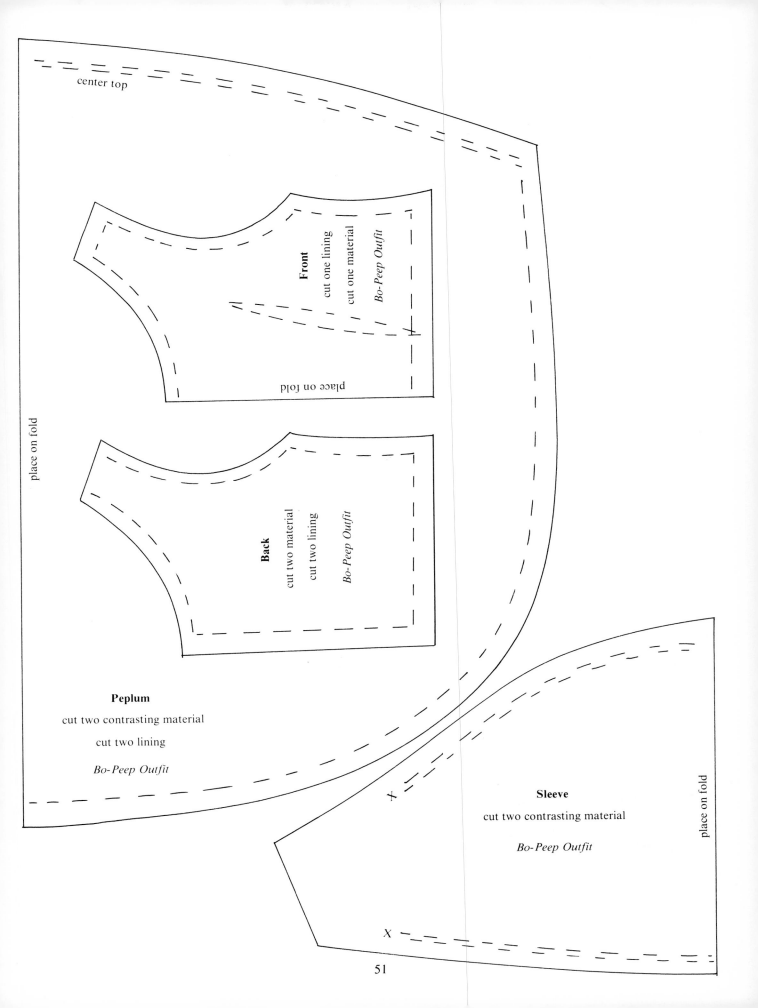

center top

place on fold

Front

cut one lining

cut one material

Bo-Peep Outfit

place on fold

Back

cut two material

cut two lining

Bo-Peep Outfit

Peplum

cut two contrasting material

cut two lining

Bo-Peep Outfit

X

Sleeve

cut two contrasting material

Bo-Peep Outfit

place on fold

X

Red Riding Hood Outfit

Materials:

Polished cotton or taffeta: 1/2yd (.46m) white
1/2yd (.46m) red
3/4yd (.69m) of 1/2in (.65cm) wide ribbon
Skirt: 5in (12.7cm) long, 30in (76.2cm) wide

See suggestions at end of instructions before purchasing fabric.

Be sure to measure garment on doll as you sew.

DRESS: FRONT: With right sides of white fabric and lining together, sew around neck edge and armholes, turn to right side. Sew two darts in front on wrong side. Clip seams along curves.

Illustration 8. Red Riding Hood outfit. *Photograph by Clifford Yeich.*

BACKS: With right sides facing, sew around neck edge and backs, turn. With right sides facing, sew shoulder seams and side seams, turn.

SKIRT: Hem bottom of skirt 1/4in (.65cm). Gather top of skirt to measure same as for bodice. Sew vents at back of skirt 2½in (6.4cm) in from top. With right sides facing, sew skirt to bodice, turn and topstitch with raw edges towards bodice. Hem back of skirt.

CAPE: With right sides of red and white material facing, sew around sides and bottom of cape and 3/4in (2cm) on each end at neck edge, turn to right side. Turn white neck edge of cape to wrong side 1/4in (.65cm) in and baste. Now turn neck edge of red piece under and baste separately, nip edges on curves.

HOOD: With white piece, fold in half, having right sides facing. Sew across top of hood. Sew red piece in same manner. Do not turn to right sides. Now insert white hood inside of red hood and sew across front of hood. All raw seams will be showing. Pull hoods apart, turn to right sides. Now insert white hood into red hood. Mark center back of hoods and center back of cape. Gather bottom of hood to measure same as top of cape between 3/4in (2cm) on each end. Insert bottom of hood to inside of top of cape about 1/4in (.65cm), baste together, then sew.

FINISHING: Tack ribbon on ends at neck edge, leaving ends to tie. Press cape and hood. Sew snaps on dress.

SUGGESTIONS: White polished cotton was used for the dress and lining. Red cotton was used for the cape and hood. Red and white taffeta can be used very effectively for both lining and fabric. □

Reprinted from the December 1984/January 1985 **Doll Reader**®.

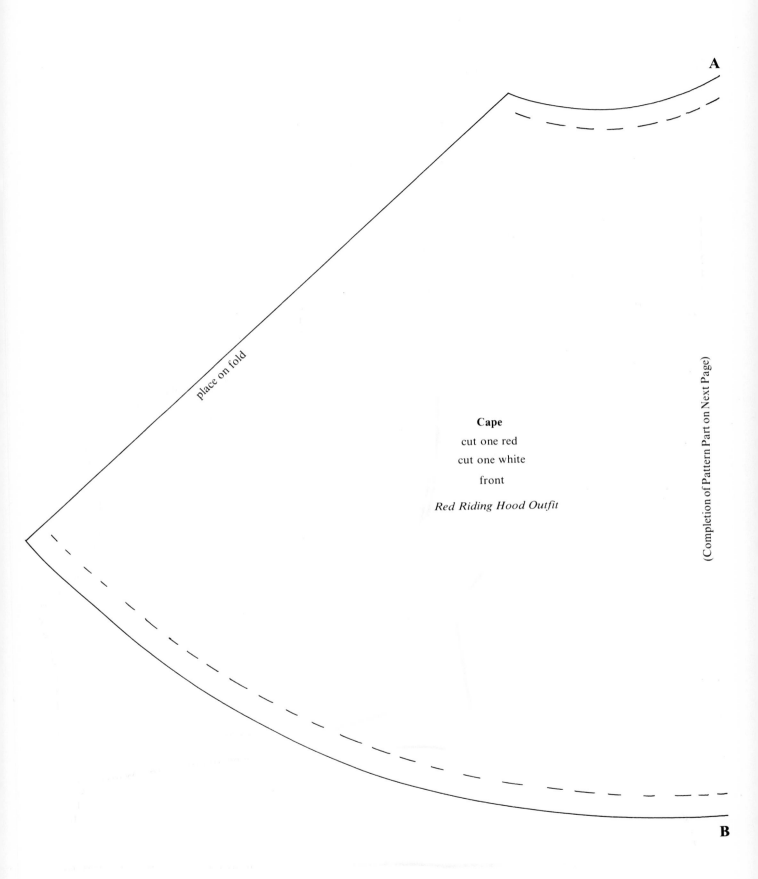

A

place on fold

Cape

cut one red

cut one white

front

Red Riding Hood Outfit

(Completion of Pattern Part on Next Page)

B

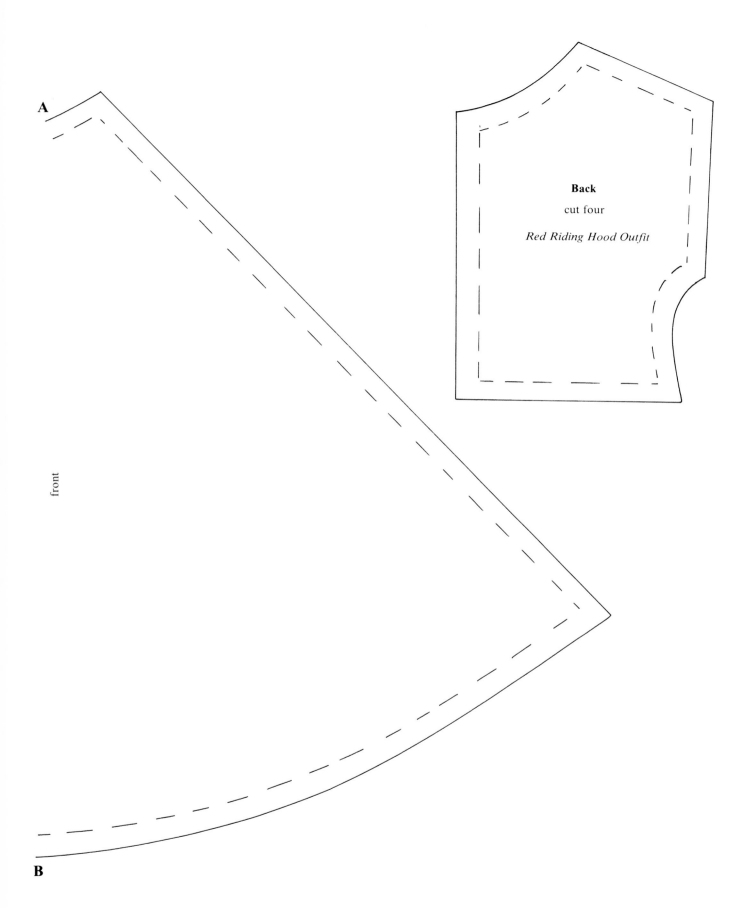

A

front

B

Back

cut four

Red Riding Hood Outfit

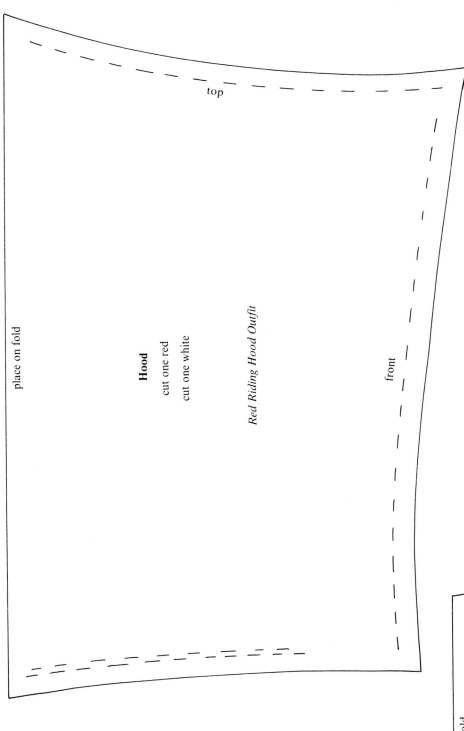

place on fold

top

Hood

cut one red

cut one white

Red Riding Hood Outfit

front

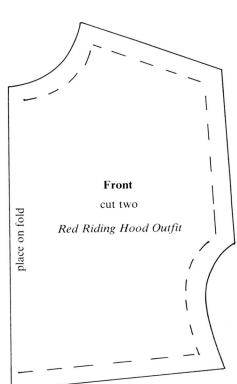

Front

cut two

Red Riding Hood Outfit

place on fold

55

Hansel Outfit

Materials:

Pants: 10in (25.4cm) long, 14in (35.6cm) wide heavy type cotton, Logan green.

Shirt: 6½in (16.5cm) long, 18in (45.7cm) wide white cotton

Straps: 14in (35.6cm) long, 1½in (3.8cm) wide

14in (35.6cm) of 1/4in (.65cm) wide braid

Stockings: 1/4yd (.23m) spandex stretch material

Be sure to measure garment on doll as you sew.

PANTS: With right sides facing, sew fronts together from top to crotch. Turn to right side and nip edges on curve. Now divide seam, topstitch closely on each side of seam. Hem bottom of legs and hem vents at back from top to crotch. Now hem top of pants under 1/2in (1.3cm) and topstitch on edge and end of hem 1/2in (1.3cm) below. Sew backs together from bottom of vents to crotch. With right sides facing, sew legs together.

STRAPS: On 14in (35.6cm) piece of straps, fold in half with right sides facing and fasten cord or narrow ribbon on end to be used later to pull to right side after sewing piece together. Be sure cord is as long as strap and do not sew fast to piece while sewing. After sewing piece together, pull to right side and press. Now sew braid in center of piece. Fasten straps after shirt is made for proper fitting.

SHIRT: Lay right sides of fronts on right side of back, sew shoulder seams. Sew two small darts in back. Sew two small darts in sleeves. Hem bottom of sleeves. Insert sleeves into armholes, easing top of sleeves. Sew underarms and side seams. Stitch ends of collar on wrong side, turn. Now baste collar on right side of shirt having notch of collar and back meet. Fold facing at notch, lay facing on top of collar and machine-stitch across top of shirt having notches meet. Stitch facing at bottom of shirt on both sides. Turn to right side and hem remaining bottom of shirt. Sew two small snaps on front.

Put pants on doll and baste straps over shoulder to fit. Fasten straps about 1/4in (.65cm) from end of back and close to seam at front of pants. Cut ends on angle for better fit. Place strap across front as shown on illustration. When all pieces fit, sew straps by hand on wrong side. Sew snap at back of pants.

KNEE SOCKS: On right side make two folds for cuff about 1/2in (1.3cm) deep on each fold. Now turn to wrong side and sew, stretching slightly as you sew and sew seam close to edge. Turn to right side. □

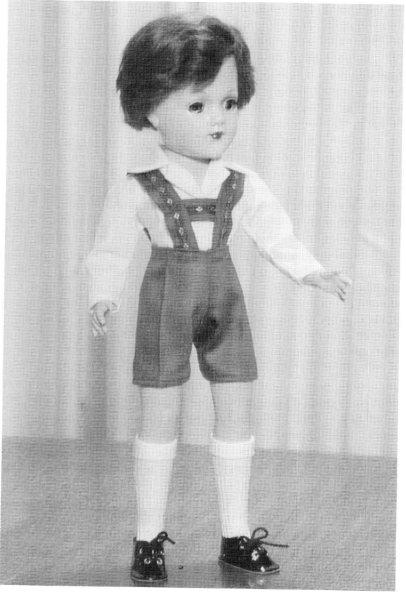

Illustration 9. Hansel outfit. *Photograph by Clifford Yeich.*

Reprinted from the February/March 1985 **Doll Reader**.

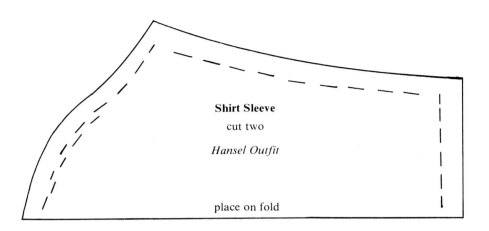

Shirt Sleeve

cut two

Hansel Outfit

place on fold

Stockings

cut two spandex stretch material

Hansel Outfit

place on fold

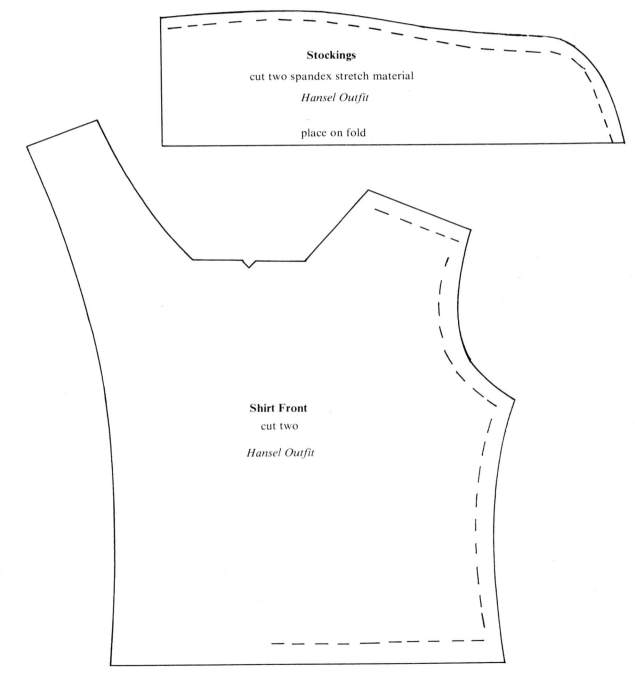

Shirt Front

cut two

Hansel Outfit

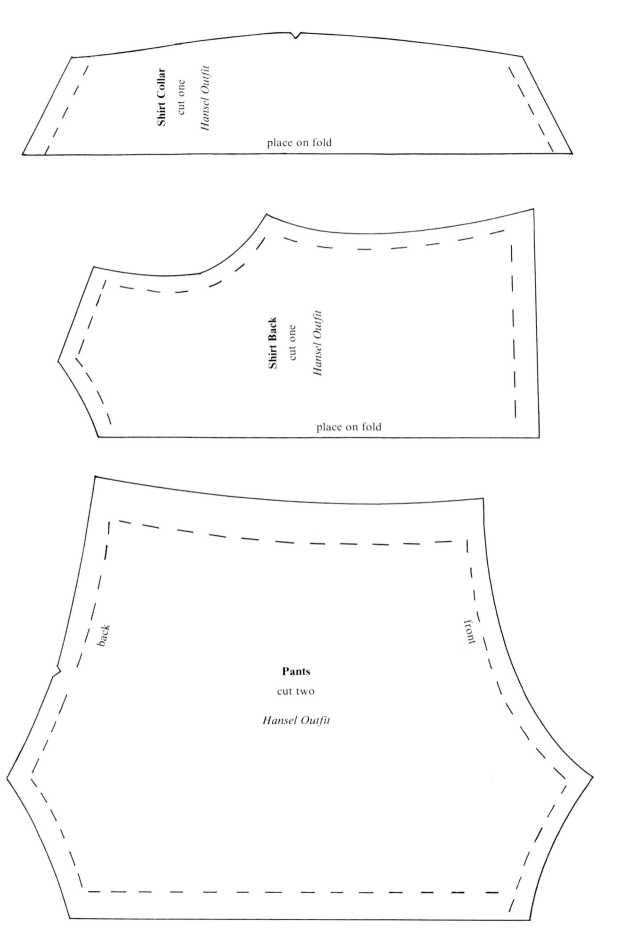

Shirt Collar
cut one
Hansel Outfit

place on fold

Shirt Back
cut one
Hansel Outfit

place on fold

back

front

Pants

cut two

Hansel Outfit

Gretel Outfit

Illustration 10. Gretel outfit. *Photograph by Clifford Yeich.*

Materials:

1/4yd (.23m) heavy type cotton, Logan green

Lightweight organdy for waistband lining

Skirt: 6in (15.2cm) long, 28in (71.1cm) wide

1¼yd (1.14m) of 1/4in (.65cm) wide braid

Straps: 11in (27.9cm) long, 1¼in (3.2cm) wide

Blouse: 5½in (14cm) long, 19in (48.3cm) wide white cotton

Neck band: 6¾in (17.2cm) long, 1in (2.5cm) wide

Sleeve bands: 3in (7.6cm) long, 1in (2.5cm) wide

Stockings: 6½in (16.5cm) long, 4in (10.2cm) wide spandex

Be sure to measure garment on doll as you sew.

SKIRT: Turn hem at bottom of skirt and sew. Sew on lace, having bottom of lace ending at bottom of skirt; do not stretch lace while sewing. Sew on braid above edge of lace as shown in illustration. Hem vents at back about 2¼in (5.8cm) from top. Gather top of skirt to fit waist loosely.

WAISTBAND: With right sides facing, lay lining on band and sew around top of band and ends, turn to right side. Sew two darts in front. With right sides facing, sew band to top of skirt; turn and topstitch on right side. Sew back of skirt together.

BLOUSE: With right sides facing, sew shoulder seams. Mark center of neck edge and gather four small pleats. Now measure 2¼in (5.8cm) below these pleats and sew four more pleats.

SLEEVES: Gather top of sleeves as shown on pattern and sew sleeves into armholes having most fullness at top of sleeve. Gather bottom of sleeve to measure 3in (7.6cm) and sew sleeve band on right side, raw edges facing. Turn band to wrong side and topstitch on right side. Sew neck band in same manner. Make two small darts in back. Sew sleeve seams and underarms. Now turn hem on backs and hem bottom of blouse.

STRAPS: With right sides facing on the 11in (27.9cm) piece of strap, fold in half and fasten cord or narrow ribbon on end (inside of strap) to be used later to pull to right side after sewing piece together. Be sure cord is as long as strap and be sure not to sew cord fast to piece while sewing. After sewing piece together, pull to right side and press. Now sew braid in center of piece. Put blouse and skirt on doll and baste straps over shoulders to fit. Cut end of straps on angle for better fit. Fasten straps close to end of skirt band about 1/4in (.65cm) and fasten front end of strap as shown in illustration. When straps are properly fitting, sew by hand on wrong side.

STOCKINGS: Fold piece in half lengthwise and, with right sides facing, sew seam on raw edges. Stretch slightly while sewing, turn to right side. When dressing doll, stretch stocking to full length of legs.

FINISHING: Sew two small snaps on blouse and one larger snap on skirt band. □

Reprinted from the April 1985 **Doll Reader**.

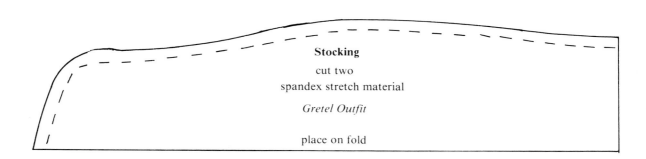

Stocking

cut two

spandex stretch material

Gretel Outfit

place on fold

Blouse Front

cut one

Gretel Outfit

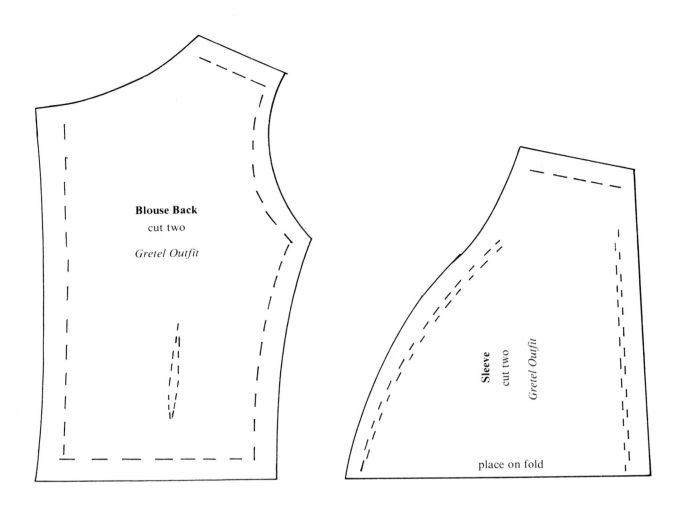

Blouse Back

cut two

Gretel Outfit

Sleeve

cut two

Gretel Outfit

place on fold

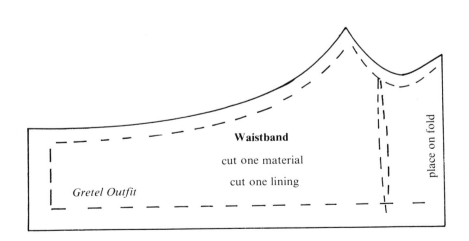

Waistband

cut one material

cut one lining

Gretel Outfit

place on fold

Snow White Outfit

Illustration 11. Snow White outfit. *Photograph by Clifford Yeich.*

Materials:

Skirt: 1/4yd (.23m) cotton

Lining for slip and bodice: 1/4yd (.23m) lightweight organdy or self-fabric

Bodice: 5in (12.7cm) long, 11in (27.9cm) wide

Sleeves: 4½in (11.5cm) long, 10in (25.4cm) wide

Skirt: 7in (17.8cm) long, 34in (86.4cm) wide

Slip: 6in (15.2cm) long, 33in (83.8cm) wide

6in (15.2cm) of 1/2in (1.3cm) wide elastic

Sleeve bands: 3in (7.6cm) long, 1in (2.5cm) wide

16in (40.6cm) long, narrow width rickrack

Be sure to measure garment on doll as you sew.

BODICE: FRONT: Lay right sides of front and right side of lining together and sew around neck edge. Nip edges on curves, turn to right side. Make two darts in front.

BACKS: Lay right sides together and sew around neck edge and backs, turn to right side. Lay backs and fronts together, right sides facing and sew shoulder seams. Sew rickrack around neck edge.

SLEEVES: Gather bottom of sleeves to measure 3in (7.6cm). Sew sleeve band on right side, turn binding over edge and topstitch close to seam. Gather top of sleeve and insert into armhole having most fullness at top of sleeve. Sew sleeve seams and side seams.

SKIRT: Hem bottom of skirt and vents at back 3¼in (8.3cm) from top. Fold skirt in half and in center measure 1/2in (1.3cm) from top and place marker. Measure 3in (7.6cm) from marker (at top of skirt), place second marker. Now cut out center from marker to marker. Mark center of bodice and center of skirt and gather top of skirt to measure same as bodice. With right sides facing, sew skirt to bodice, be sure centers meet. Do not have too much fullness at center of skirt. Turn to right side and topstitch having raw edges toward bodice. Hem back of skirt.

SLIP: Hem bottom and mark center of slip. Gather top of skirt to measure about 15in (38.1cm). Mark center of elastic and sew to top of slip, stretching elastic as you sew, having centers meet. Sew back of slip. □

Reprinted from the May 1985 **Doll Reader**®.

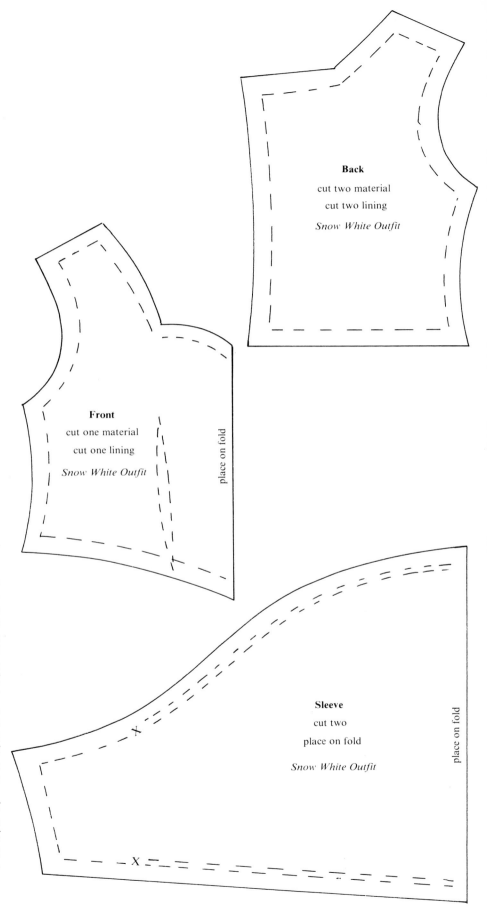

Miss Muffet Outfit

Illustration 12. Miss Muffet outfit. *Photograph by Clifford Yeich.*

Materials:

Dress and pantaloons: 1/3yd (.30m) pink checked gingham (use checked gingham for lining also)

1/4yd (.23m) eyelet

3yd (2.73m) eyelet trim

Skirt: 4½in (11.5cm) long, 32in (81.3cm) wide

Skirt ruffle: 2in (5.1cm) long, 1¾yd (1.6m) wide

Eyelet skirt: 4½in (11.5cm) long, 32in (81.3cm) wide

1½yd (1.36m) of 1in (2.5cm) wide eyelet skirt trim

1¼yd (1.14m) of 1in (2.5cm) wide eyelet pantaloon trim

Sleeve bands: 3in (7.6cm) long, 1in (2.5cm) wide

5in (12.7cm) of 1/4in (.65cm) wide elastic

Be sure to measure garment on doll as you sew.

BODICE: Place front piece of lining on right side of bodice and sew around neck edge, turn. Place lining on right side of backs and sew around neck edge and backs, turn. Sew two darts in front of bodice. With right sides facing, sew shoulder seams.

SLEEVES: Gather bottom of sleeve between x's to measure 3in (7.6cm). Sew on sleeve bands with raw edges meeting. Now turn edge under 1/4in (.65cm) and on wrong side, topstitch. Gather top of sleeve between x's and insert into armholes, having most fullness at top of sleeve. Sew sleeve seams and side seams.

SKIRT RUFFLE: With main color, hem bottom of piece.

SKIRT: With right sides facing, gather on ruffle, turn and topstitch.

EYELET SKIRT: With right sides facing, gather eyelet trim on bottom of eyelet skirt, turn and topstitch. Mark center of each skirt. Now gather skirts together (having centers meet), to measure same as for bodice and hem vents on skirts about 3in (7.6cm) from top. With right sides facing, sew skirts to bodice, turn and topstitch. Hem back of skirts.

PANTALOONS: Sew fronts together with right sides facing from top to crotch. Hem 1/4in (.65cm) at top and sew elastic on wrong side, stretching while sewing. Hem bottom of legs. Now gather three rows of eyelet trim on bottom of pantaloons, having first row of trim extending 1/4in (.65cm) over hem at bottom. Gather two more rows, having trim overlap about 1/4in (.65cm) above. Now sew backs together from top to crotch. With right sides facing, sew legs together.

Sew snaps on bodice. □

Reprinted from the June/July 1985 **Doll Reader**®.

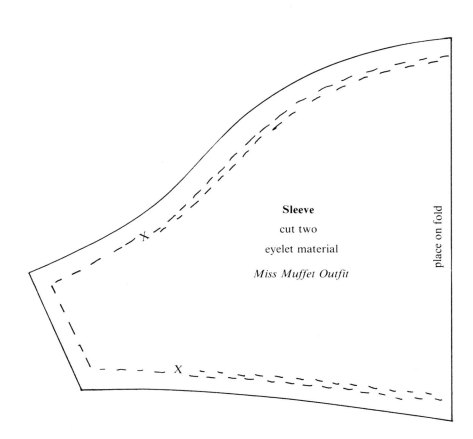

Sleeve

cut two

eyelet material

Miss Muffet Outfit

place on fold

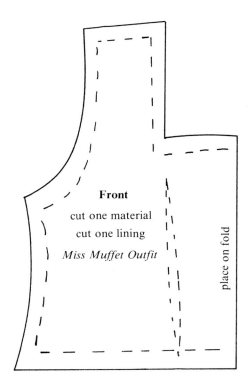

Front

cut one material

cut one lining

Miss Muffet Outfit

place on fold

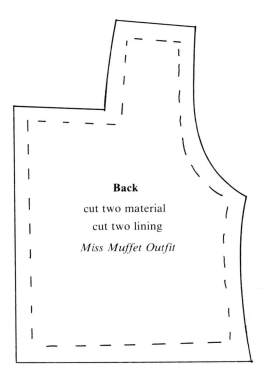

Back

cut two material

cut two lining

Miss Muffet Outfit

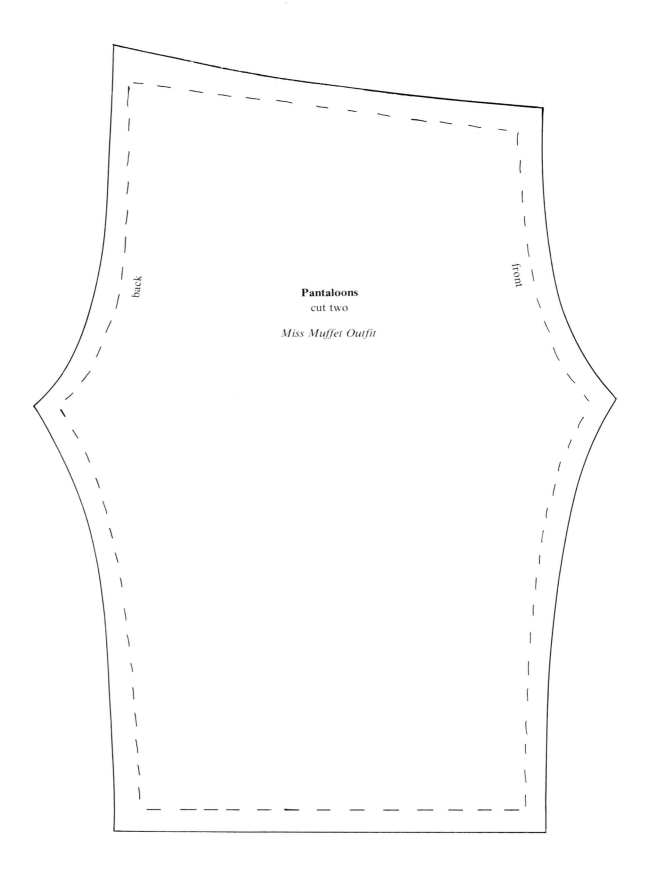

Pantaloons
cut two

Miss Muffet Outfit

back

front

Fairy Princess Outfit

Illustration 13. Fairy Princess outfit. *Photograph by Clifford Yeich.*

Materials:

Dress: 1/3yd (.30m) taffeta

1/3yd (.30m) stiff nylon net flecked with silver

Crown lining: 9in (22.9cm) long, 7in (17.8cm) wide buckram

Elastic: 5in (12.7cm) long, 1/2in (1.3cm) wide for slip; 1½in (3.8cm) long, 1/2in (1.3cm) wide for crown

Slip: 1/4yd (.23m) organdy

Taffeta skirt: 8¾in (22.3cm) long, 34in (86.4cm) wide

Net skirt: 9¼in (23.6cm) long, 36in (91.4cm) wide

Slip: 8in (20.3cm) long, 33in (83.8cm) wide

Be sure to measure garment on doll as you sew.

BODICE: Place front piece of net under wrong side of bodice and sew around neck edge, turn to right side. Place net under wrong side of backs and sew around neck edge and backs, turn. Sew two darts in front of bodice. With right sides of front and backs facing, sew shoulder seams. Sew on braid starting at neck edge on back and front of bodice as shown in the illustration.

SLEEVES: Gather top of net sleeves between x's, having most fullness at top of sleeve. Gather bottom of sleeve to measure 3in (7.6cm). On right side of sleeve sew on band, turn under and topstitch on right side. Sew braid on top of band. Insert sleeve into armhole and sew sleeve seams and side seams.

SKIRTS: Hem bottom of taffeta skirt and vents at back about 4in (10.2cm) from top. Now hem bottom of net skirt and sew on braid. Stretch net skirt slightly while sewing on braid. Mark center of each skirt and lay net skirt on right side of taffeta skirt and gather skirts together to measure same as for bodice, easing net skirt as you gather. Be sure to have centers meet. Mark center of skirt and center of bodice. With right sides facing, sew skirts to bodice; do not have too much fullness in center of skirts. Turn to right side and topstitch, having raw edges toward bodice. Sew braid around waist. Make a small bow and streamers with braid as shown in the illustration. Sew back of skirts separately.

SLIP: Hem bottom of slip and gather top of slip to measure about 15in (38.1cm). Mark center of slip and center of elastic and sew elastic over gathers, stretching elastic while sewing. Sew back of slip.

CROWN: With right sides facing, sew ends and top of crown together, turn to right side. Sew two pieces of buckram together. Now insert buckram inside of crown and turn front edge of crown over buckram and baste. Turn back piece of crown under and baste, sew together. Sew braid completely around crown. Sew elastic on ends of crown to fit head, turn elastic under on wrong side while sewing. Paste on rhinestones. □

Reprinted from the August/September 1985 **Doll Reader**®.

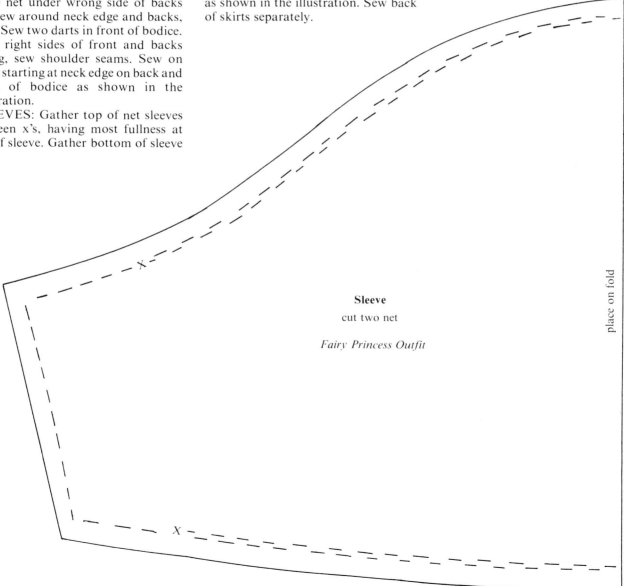

Sleeve

cut two net

Fairy Princess Outfit

place on fold

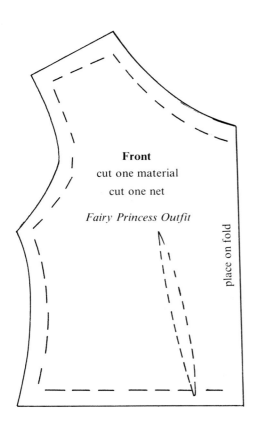

Front

cut one material

cut one net

Fairy Princess Outfit

place on fold

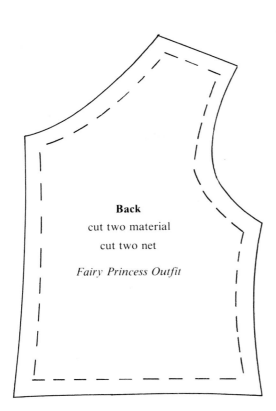

Back

cut two material

cut two net

Fairy Princess Outfit

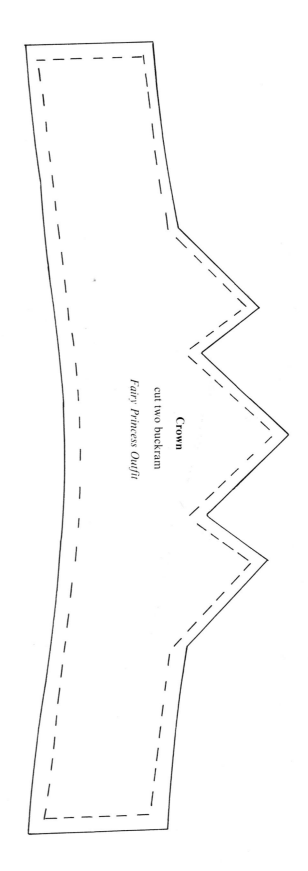

Crown

cut two buckram

Fairy Princess Outfit

Miss Mars Outfit

Materials:

1/3yd (.30m) lightweight fabric, woven with gold thread

Lining: 1/3yd (.30m) lightweight crepe fabric

Skirt: 8¾in (22.3cm) long, 36in (91.4cm) wide

Lining: 8¾in (22.3cm) long, 36in (91.4cm) wide

Slip: 8in (20.3cm) long, 34in (86.4cm) wide

6¼in (15.9cm) of 1/4in (.65cm) wide elastic

Be sure to measure garment on doll as you sew.

BODICE: There are two fronts, two linings, four backs and four linings. Lay lining on wrong side of two fronts. Lay lining on wrong side of four backs. With right sides facing, lay two of the backs on one front (with linings). Pin or baste in place and sew shoulder seams. Now press shoulder seams open. Work other front and backs in same manner. With right sides facing, lay these two sets together. Baste or pin in place having shoulder seams meet. Sew completely around backs, shoulders and front. Turn to right side and press lightly. Baste darts in front and backs, baste side seams. Try on doll and adjust darts to fit. Be sure back of bodice has about 1/2in (1.3cm) overlap for closing. Sew darts and take out basting.

SLEEVE BINDINGS: With right sides facing, sew binding around armholes. Turn under and topstitch on right side, nip edges. Sew side seams.

SKIRT: With right sides facing, sew skirt and lining together on bottom; turn to right side, press lightly on wrong side. Hem vents at back about 3½in (8.9cm) from top. Measure center of skirt and center of bodice. Gather top of skirt to fit bodice. With right sides facing, sew skirt to bodice. Try not to have as much gathers at front between darts. Press raw seams toward bodice and topstitch. Sew back of skirt to vent. Sew one large snap on bodice. Place gown on doll and gather about 1/2in (1.3cm) at center front or make a small pleat. Turn down top of gown as shown in illustration.

SLIP: Hem bottom of slip. Mark center of slip and center of elastic. Gather top of slip to measure 16in (40.6cm) wide. Now gather slip with elastic, stretching elastic as you sew. Sew back of slip together. □

Illustration 14. Miss Mars. *Photograph by Clifford Yeich.*

Reprinted from the November 1985 **Doll Reader**.

70

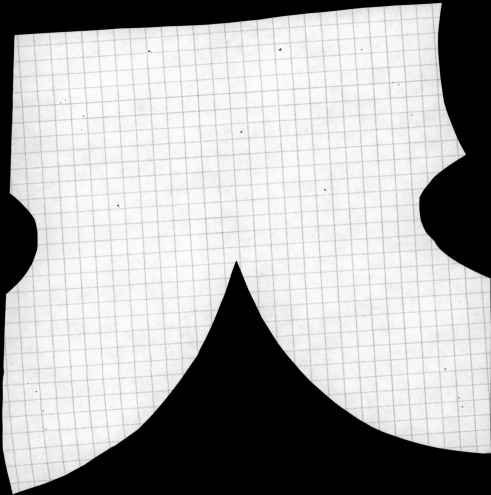

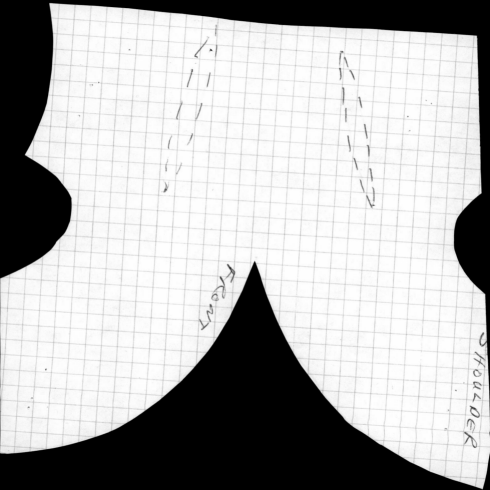

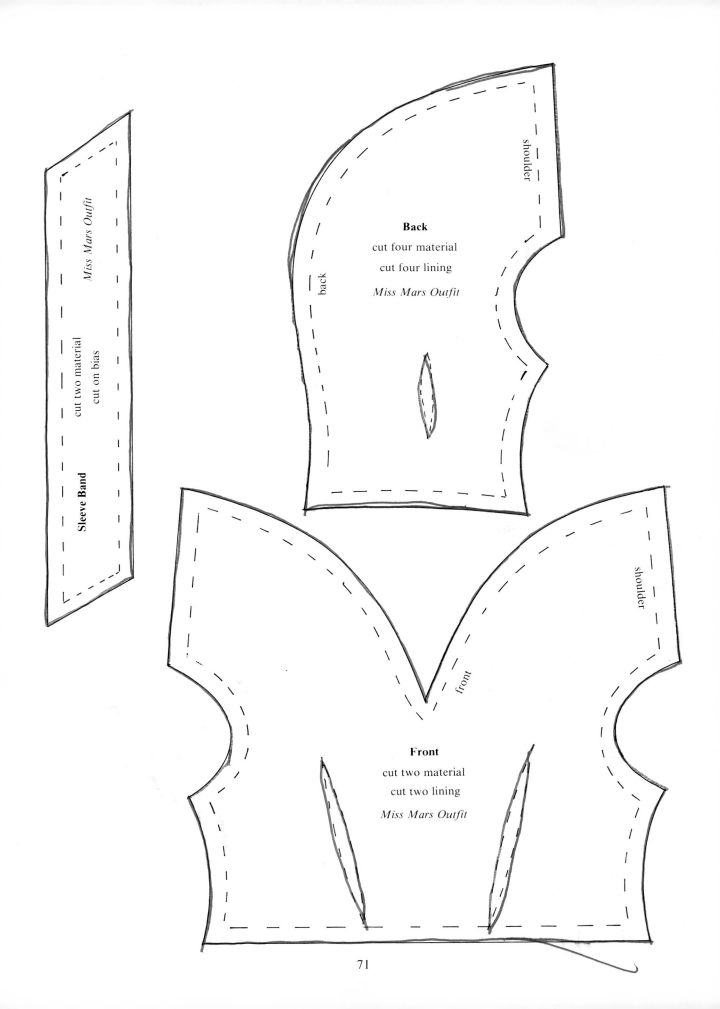

Sleeve Band

cut two material

cut on bias

Miss Mars Outfit

Back

cut four material

cut four lining

Miss Mars Outfit

shoulder

back

Front

cut two material

cut two lining

Miss Mars Outfit

shoulder

front

Miss Jupiter Outfit

Illustration 15. Miss Jupiter. *Photograph by Scott Hime.*

Materials:

1/2yd (.46m) taffeta or lightweight satin

1yd (.91m) sheer tricot or fine mesh nylon net

Satin skirt: 8¾in (22.3cm) long, 40in (101.6cm) wide

Tricot skirt: 9in (22.9cm) long, 46in (116.8cm) wide

Skirt ruffle: 4yd (3.64m) long, 4½in (11.5cm) wide

Neck ruffle: 2yd (1.82m) long, 1¾in (4.5cm) wide

Small handmade rosebuds: one dozen

See suggestions before purchasing fabric.

Be sure to measure garment on doll as you sew.

FRONT: Lay lining on wrong side of front, sew around neck edge and armholes, nip edges, turn to right side. Sew two darts in front on wrong side.

BACKS: Lay lining on wrong side of backs and sew around neck edge, backs and armholes. Nip edges and turn to right sides, sew darts. With right sides facing, sew shoulder seams. Gather ruffle and sew ruffle around neck edge. Sew side seams. Place bodice on doll and cut off 1/4in (.65cm) ruffle across front, leaving ruffle on shoulders and back a little longer.

SKIRT: Hem bottom of satin skirt. Hem vents at back on satin and sheer skirt separately, about 3¼in (8.3cm) from top. Now sew ruffle on bottom of tricot skirt leaving ruffle extended 1/2in (1.3cm) below bottom of tricot skirt. Mark center of tricot skirt and satin skirt. Lay tricot on right side of satin and gather skirts together easing tricot as you sew. Do not ease tricot at front of skirt. Mark center of bodice and gather skirts to measure same as bodice. With right sides facing, sew skirts to bodice, turn to right side and topstitch. Sew back of satin and tricot skirt separately to vents. Sew two snaps on bodice. Trim skirt and shoulder ruffle with small rosebuds as shown in the illustration.

SUGGESTIONS: The gown shown in the illustration was made with soft satin and sheer tricot nylon. This gown can be made in taffeta and fine mesh nylon very effectively and is a little easier to sew. If small handmade rosebuds cannot be obtained, small narrow bows may be made with narrow satin or velvet ribbon. □

Reprinted from the February/March 1986 **Doll Reader**.

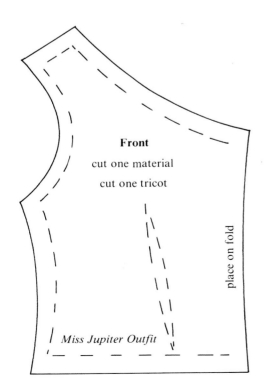

Front

cut one material

cut one tricot

place on fold

Miss Jupiter Outfit

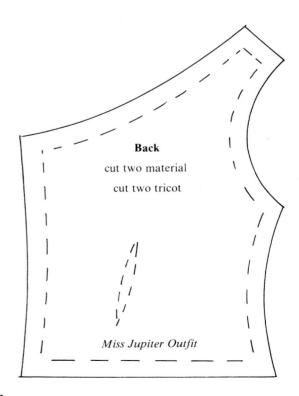

Back

cut two material

cut two tricot

Miss Jupiter Outfit

Miss Saturn Outfit

Illustration 16. Miss Saturn. *Photograph by Scott Hime.*

Materials:
3/4yd (.69m) skinner satin
3/4yd (.69m) white nylon net
Sequins: 42in (106.6cm) of each, royal
  purple and gold
Slip: 1/2yd (.46m) organdy
Band for slip: 6½in (16.5cm) by 1¼in
  (3.2cm)

See suggestions at end of instructions before purchasing fabric.

Be sure to measure garment on doll as you sew.

BODICE: Lay net on right side of satin and sew ends and top of bodice. Turn to right side and press lightly on wrong side. Sew darts on wrong side as shown on chart. Now sew gold sequins on right side of bodice. Sequins can be sewn on by hand or machine-stitched. Pin sequins in place and stitch on wrong side of bodice. Do not sew ends.

SKIRTS: Hem bottom of satin skirt. Hem vents at back of satin and net skirts separately, about 4in (10.2cm) long as shown on pattern. Transfer pattern on short net skirt and pin gold sequins in place. Pins will be on wrong side. Turn to wrong side and stitch by hand or glue sequins, being careful not to get glue on net. Now pin purple sequins over gold as shown on illustration. Mark centers of skirts and lay long net skirt over satin, lay short net skirt over net skirt and satin, being sure centers meet. Baste together, starting at center, then machine-stitch. Mark center of bodice and, with right sides facing, baste skirts to bodice starting at center front. Now machine-stitch on wrong side, turn to right side and topstitch, turning raw edges toward bodice. Hem back of skirts to vents, hemming each skirt separately. Sew back of satin and long net skirt together. Now sew ends of net skirt with sequins together.

SLIP: This circular slip has four inverted pleats. Fold line one over line two, forming a pleat. Make three more pleats in the same manner. Sew both sides of pleats.

BAND: Lay right side of band on right side of slip and sew together. Now turn raw edge under and sew on wrong side. Hem bottom of slip and sew vents at back. Sew back of slip together on wrong side.

FINISHING: Sew one small snap at top of bodice and a larger snap at bottom. Sew a small snap on the band of the slip.

SUGGESTIONS: Sequins on the gown can be flat or cup. Flat sequins were used in this gown. Satin fabric was also used but taffeta is very effective. If taffeta is used it should be woven or of firm texture. Net should be a fine mesh and of firm texture. □

Reprinted from the April 1986 **Doll Reader**.

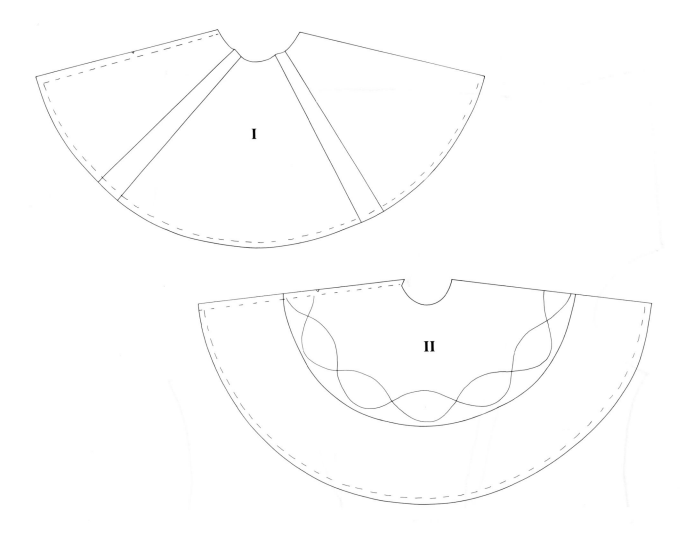

The slip and skirt patterns for Miss Saturn are single-piece patterns. However, because of the large size of these patterns, each is presented here as three separate pieces to be assembled. Small drawings of the complete slip pattern (I) as well as the skirt pattern (II) are both shown here. To create the slip pattern, simply trace and cut out the three pieces for pattern I. Place the gray line from A to B directly on top of the gray line from A to B on the second piece and tape the two pieces together. In the same manner, place the gray line from C to D on top of the gray line from C to D on the remaining piece and tape these pieces together to complete the pattern. The skirt pattern (II) is assembled in the same fashion by aligning matching letters.

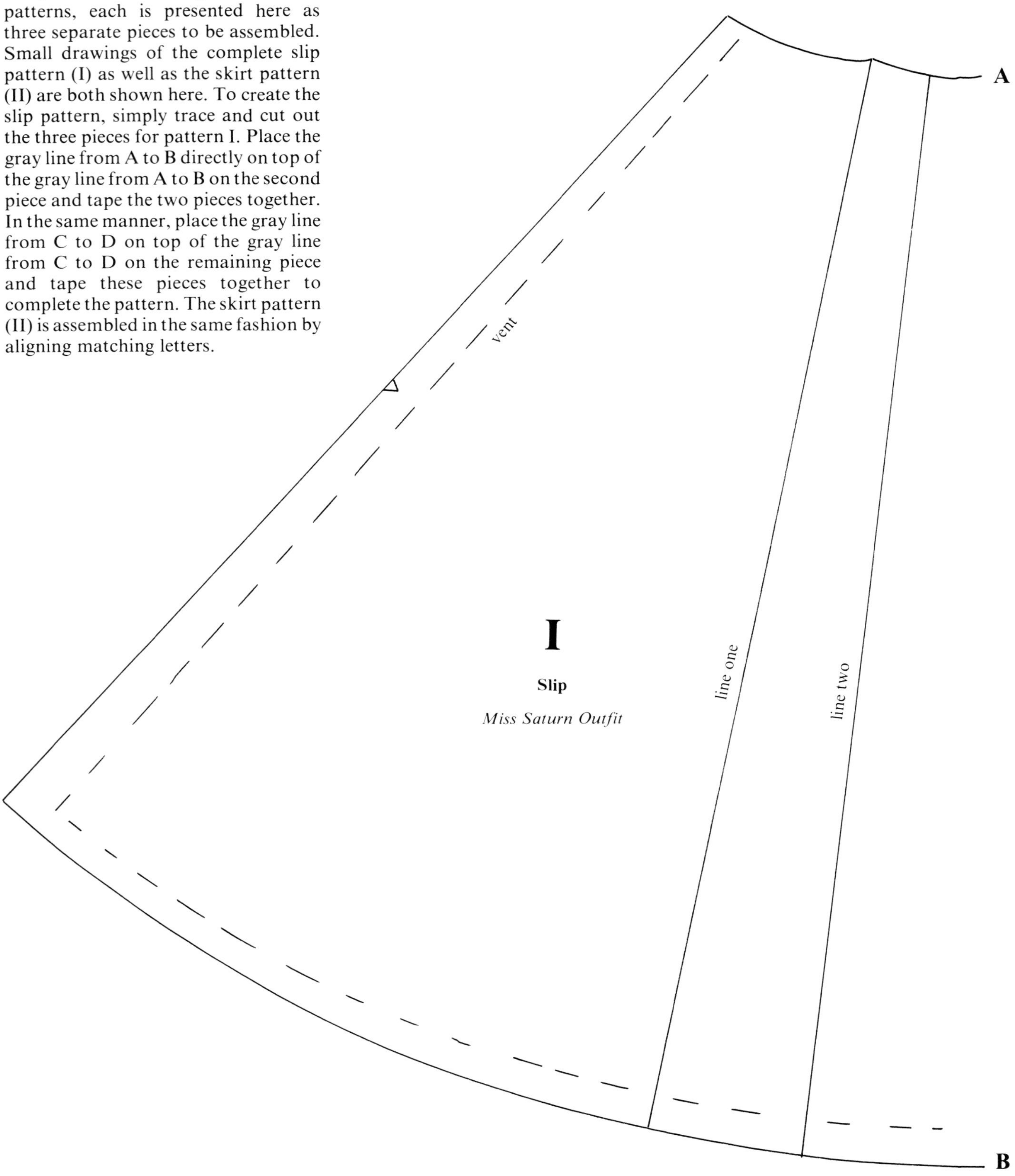

vent

A

I

Slip

Miss Saturn Outfit

line one

line two

B

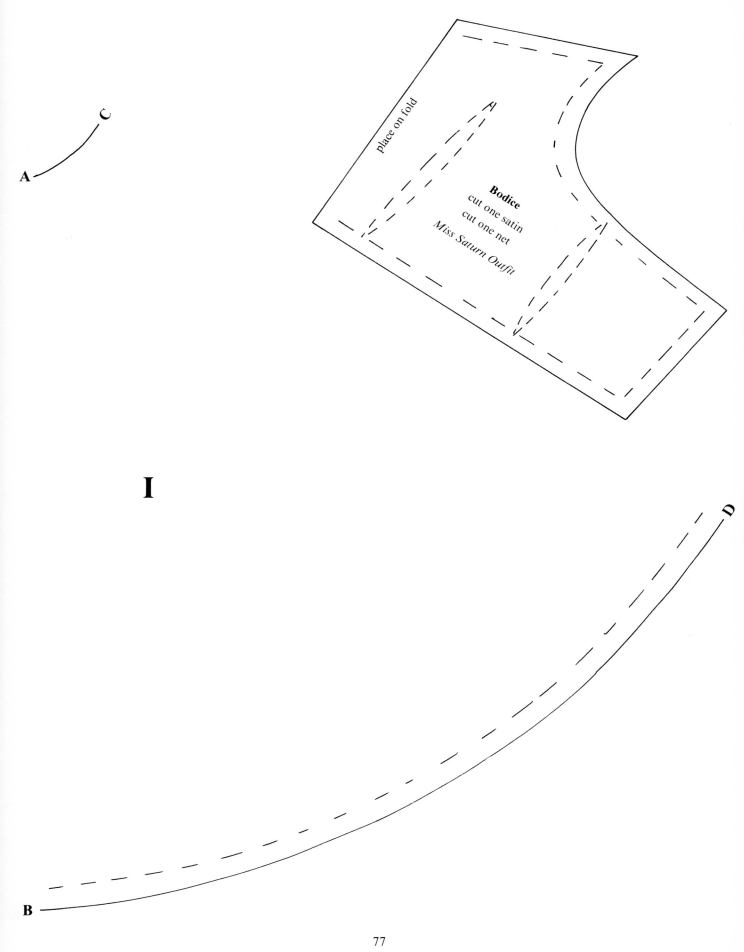

C

A

place on fold

Bodice
cut one satin
cut one net
Miss Saturn Outfit

I

D

B

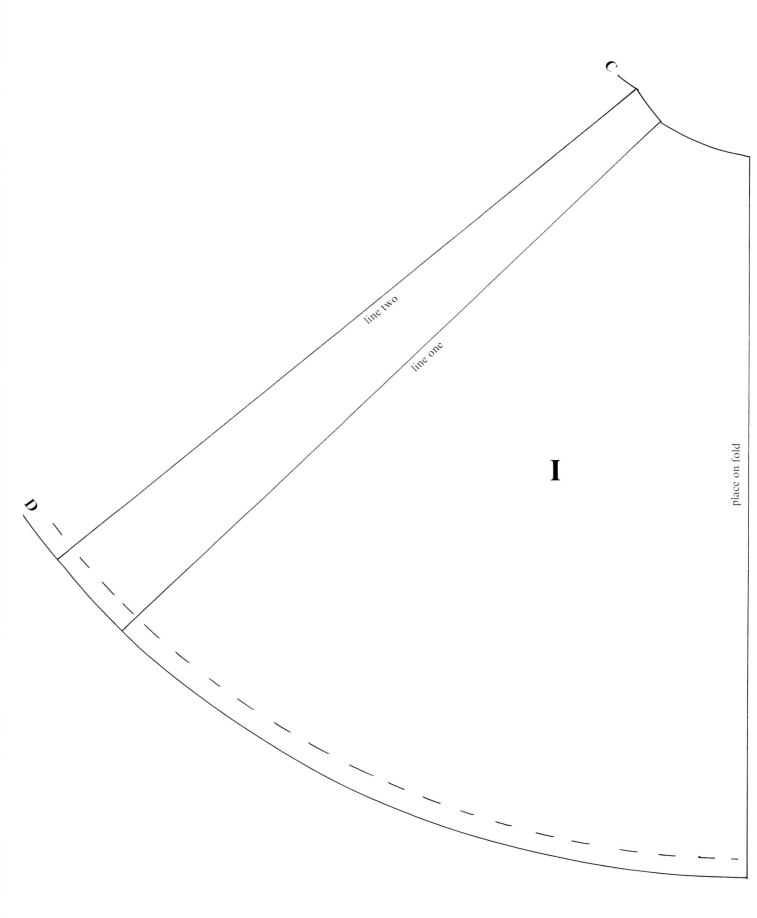

line two

line one

C

D

I

place on fold

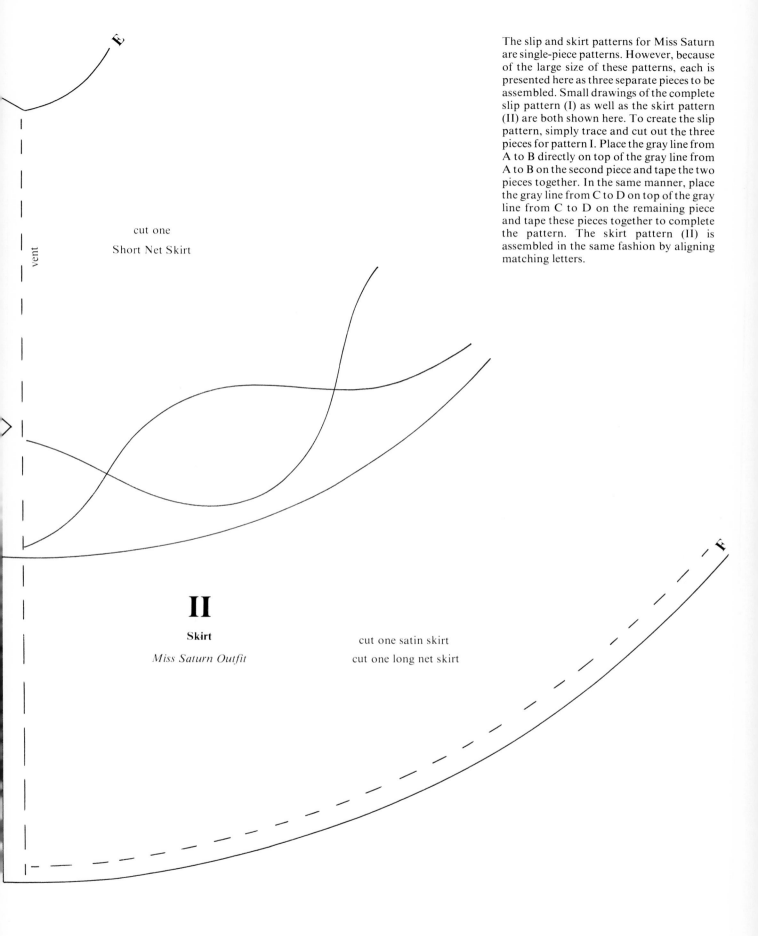

E

vent

cut one
Short Net Skirt

The slip and skirt patterns for Miss Saturn are single-piece patterns. However, because of the large size of these patterns, each is presented here as three separate pieces to be assembled. Small drawings of the complete slip pattern (I) as well as the skirt pattern (II) are both shown here. To create the slip pattern, simply trace and cut out the three pieces for pattern I. Place the gray line from A to B directly on top of the gray line from A to B on the second piece and tape the two pieces together. In the same manner, place the gray line from C to D on top of the gray line from C to D on the remaining piece and tape these pieces together to complete the pattern. The skirt pattern (II) is assembled in the same fashion by aligning matching letters.

F

II

Skirt

Miss Saturn Outfit

cut one satin skirt
cut one long net skirt

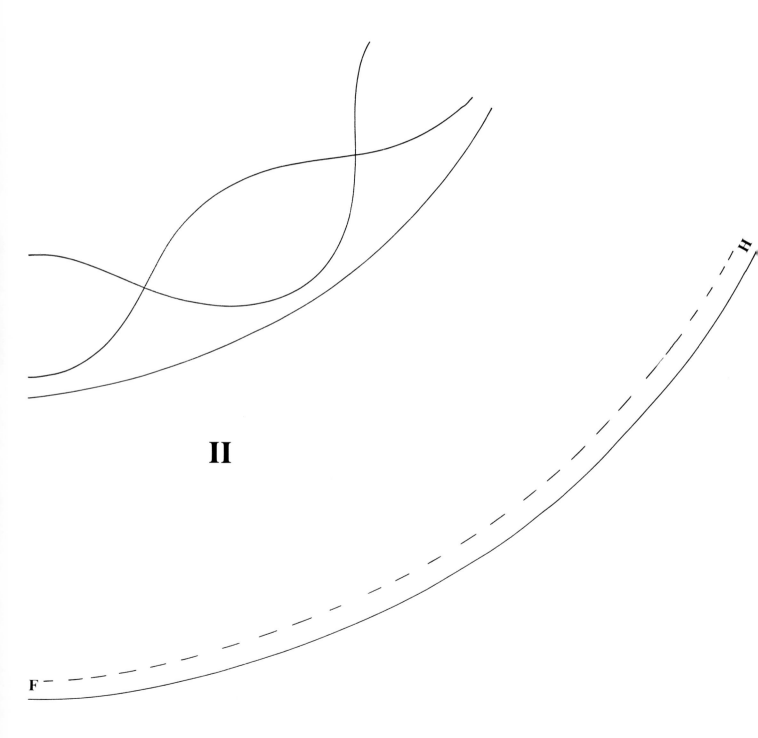

II

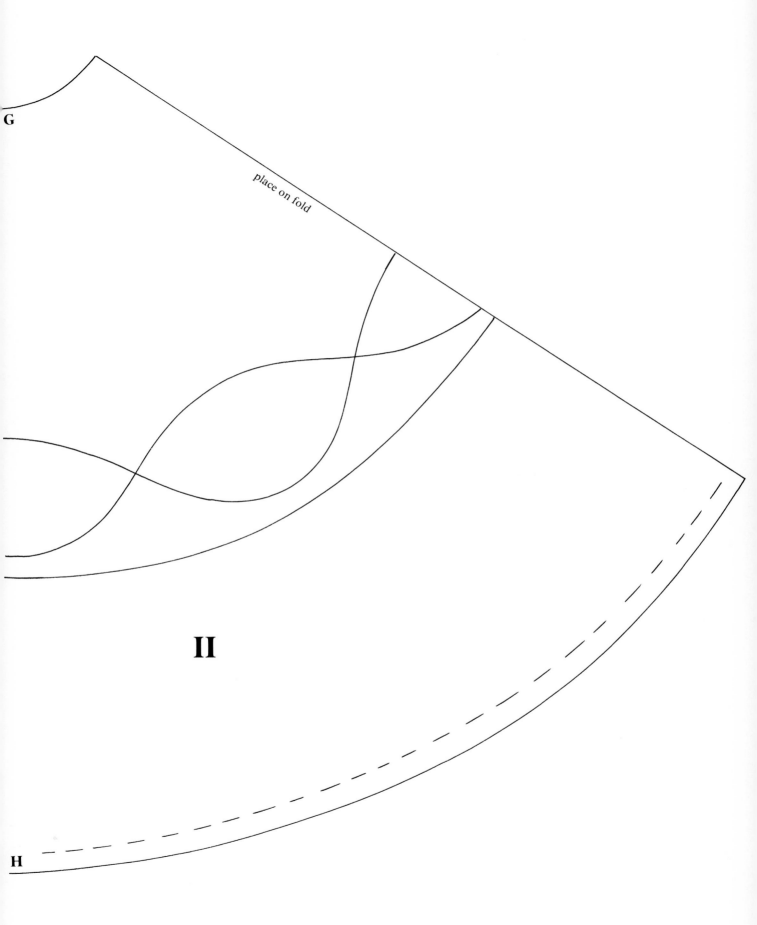

G

place on fold

II

H

Miss Uranus Outfit

Illustration 17. Miss Uranus. *Photograph by Scott Hime.*

Materials:

1/3yd (.3m) lightweight satin
1/4yd (.23m) white lace
1/4yd (.23m) nylon net, lining for jacket and slip
6in (15.2cm) long, 1/2in (1.3cm) wide elastic
Two small pearl or rhinestone buttons
Satin skirt: 8¾in (22.3cm) long, 44in (111.7cm) wide
Slip: top of slip - 4¼in (10.9cm) long, 22in (55.9cm) wide
Ruffle to slip: 5½in (14cm) long, 36in (91.4cm)
Bands on sleeves: 3in (7.6cm) long, 1in (2.5cm) wide satin

See suggestions at end of instructions before purchasing fabric.

Be sure to measure garment on doll as you sew.

DRESS: BODICE: Lay net on right side of front and sew around neck edge and armholes, turn to right side. Sew darts as shown on pattern.

BACKS: Lay net on right side of backs and sew around neck edge, backs and armholes. Turn to right side and sew small darts. With right sides facing, lay backs on front, sew shoulder seams and side seams.

SKIRT: Measure 1in (2.5cm) from each end of skirt, place pin. This will be the top of your skirt, 42in (106.6cm) wide. From the marker to the bottom of the skirt, 44in (111.7cm) wide, cut slanting ends.

Hem bottom of skirt. Mark center of skirt at top and bottom. Measure 2½in (6.4cm) from each marker. Now make a pleat by folding top marker to center marker at top of skirt and fasten with pin.

On bottom marker pin to within 1/2in (1.3cm) from marker (first pleat). Now measure 2½in (6.4cm) from fold of first pleat (at center pin), place pin at top of skirt. On bottom of skirt measure 2½in (6.4cm) from fold of first pleat, place pin.

Now fold second pleat in same manner. Place top fold of pleat 1/4in (.65cm) from fold of last pleat and bottom fold of pleat to within 1in (2.5cm) of previous fold.

Continue in this manner to end of skirt. Adjust last pleat so you will have 1/4in (.65cm) for vent at back. First half of pleated skirt should measure about 3½in (8.9cm).

Make pleats on other half of skirt in same manner, folding pleats toward the center. Adjust pleats slightly if necessary to fit bodice.

Now sew across top of skirt. Take out pins and press lightly on wrong side. With right sides facing, baste skirt to bodice, starting at center of bodice and skirt. Now sew together. Turn to right side and topstitch, turning raw edges toward bodice. Sew vents at back and sew back of skirt together.

SLIP: Fold the 5½in (14cm) long ruffle in half, mark center of ruffle and pin raw edges in place. Mark center of top piece of slip and, with raw edges facing, gather ruffle to top piece of slip, having centers meet. Turn and topstitch on wrong side, turning raw edges toward top of slip. Mark center top of slip and gather to measure about 14in (35.6cm). Mark center of elastic and sew elastic over gathers on right side, having centers meet. Stretch elastic while sewing. Sew back of slip together on wrong side.

LACE JACKET: FRONT: Lay net on right side of front and sew around front edge. Work second front to correspond, turn to right side. Sew small darts as shown on pattern.

BACK: Lay net on right side of back and sew around neck edge, turn, clip edges on curve. Make two small darts as shown on pattern. With right sides facing, lay fronts on back and sew shoulder seams.

SLEEVES: Lay lace over net and pin in place. Mark center at top of sleeve and make three small pleats. Gather bottom of sleeve to measure 3in (7.6cm). Now sew sleeve band on bottoms of sleeves as follows: Lay right sides of band on right side of lace, sew together. Turn to wrong side and turn raw edges under, sew across bottom of sleeve. Make small darts as shown on pattern. Insert sleeves into armholes having fullness in center of armhole. Clip edges around armholes.

PEPLUM: Lay net on right side of lace and sew around circular piece, turn to right side. Now sew across top of piece. Mark center of peplum at top and center of bodice at back, baste together starting at center back, then machine-stitch. Turn to right side and topstitch, turning raw edges toward bodice.

FINISHING: Sew two small snaps on bodice of gown. Sew small hook and eye at waistline of jacket and sew two small buttons as shown on illustration.

SUGGESTIONS: The fabric used in the gown shown here was cross star taffeta, 45in (114.3cm) wide. The lace in the jacket was embossed lace and net was used for the lining. If you use a lighter weight all-over lace for the jacket, the dress material may be used effectively as lining for the jacket. The net used was a fine mesh and firm. □

Reprinted from the May 1986 **Doll Reader®**.

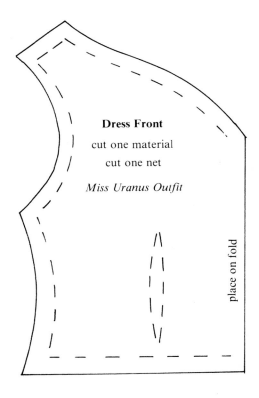

Dress Front

cut one material

cut one net

Miss Uranus Outfit

place on fold

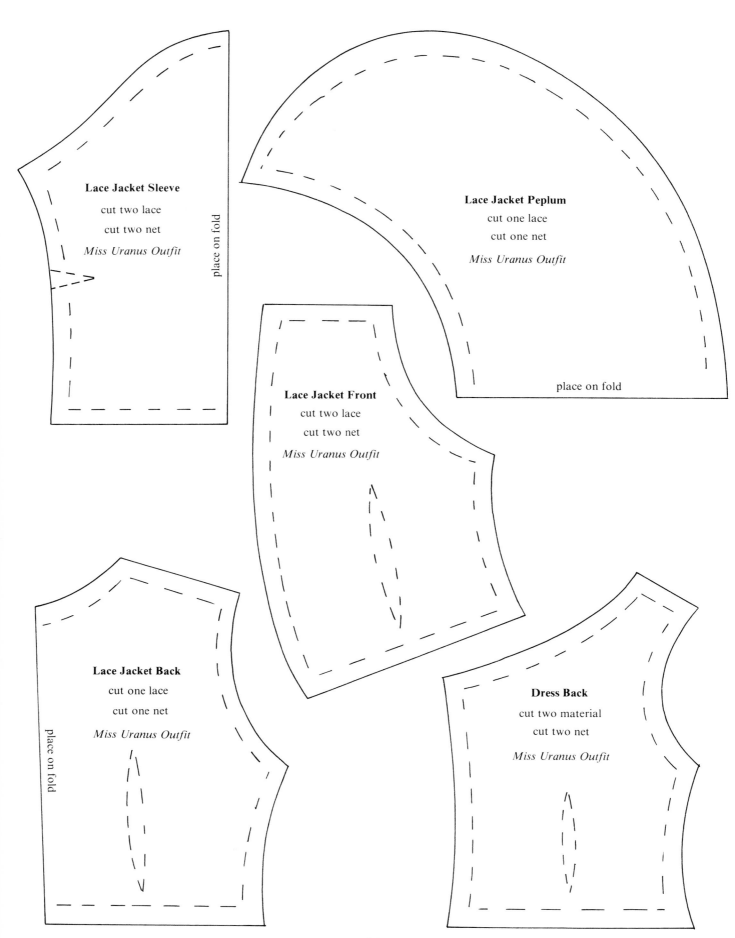

Lace Jacket Sleeve

cut two lace

cut two net

Miss Uranus Outfit

place on fold

Lace Jacket Peplum

cut one lace

cut one net

Miss Uranus Outfit

place on fold

Lace Jacket Front

cut two lace

cut two net

Miss Uranus Outfit

Lace Jacket Back

cut one lace

cut one net

Miss Uranus Outfit

place on fold

Dress Back

cut two material

cut two net

Miss Uranus Outfit

Miss Neptune Outfit

Illustration 18. Miss Neptune. *Photograph by Scott Hime.*

Materials:

3/4yd (.69m) satin or woven taffeta
3/4yd (.69m) nylon net
120 small pearls
5in (12.7cm) of 1/2in (1.3cm) wide elastic
Net scarf: 25in (63.5cm) long, 11in (27.9cm) wide
Slip: 1/2yd (.46m) firm net or organdy
Top of slip: 4½in (11.5cm) long, 38in (96.5cm) wide
Ruffle to slip: 6in (15.2cm) long, 64in (162.5cm) wide

See suggestions at end of instructions before purchasing fabric.
Be sure to measure garment on doll as you sew.

BODICE: Lay net on wrong side of bodice and sew around backs and top of bodice. Clip edges and turn to right side. Sew darts as shown on pattern.

NET SKIRT: Starting at bottom of net, sew pearls across row as follows: Gather three small stitches as shown on pattern, draw together and insert bead through needle, fasten to gathered end. Stitch through bead several times and fasten thread securely on wrong side. Continue working across row in same manner and throughout skirt as marked on pattern.

SATIN SKIRT: Hem bottom of skirt and vents on skirts separately. Lay right side of net skirt on right side of satin skirt and sew together. Now mark center of bodice and center of skirts. Gather skirts to fit bodice. With right sides facing, sew skirts to bodice, having centers meet. Turn to right side and topstitch. Sew back of skirts together, separately. Gather one end of scarf and sew between net and satin on left shoulder. Sew beads on bodice.

SLIP: Fold the 64in (162.5cm) wide ruffle piece in half, 3in (7.6cm), mark center of ruffle and pin raw edges together. Mark center of top piece of slip, having centers meet. Turn and topstitch on wrong side turning raw edges toward top of slip. Mark center top of slip and gather to measure about 14in (35.6cm). Mark center of elastic and sew elastic over gathers, having centers meet. Stretch elastic while sewing. Sew back of slip together on wrong side.

FINISHING: Sew two snaps on bodies, a small snap at the top of the bodice and a larger snap at the waist. Drape net scarf over doll's head and right arm as shown in the illustration.

SUGGESTIONS: Firm satin and net was used in the gown shown in the illustration. However, taffeta and a softer net may be used effectively but then a slip should be used to show off the skirt. The slip should be made of firm material. The colors green or blue excellent choices for Miss Neptune. □

Reprinted from the June/July 1986 **Doll Reader**.

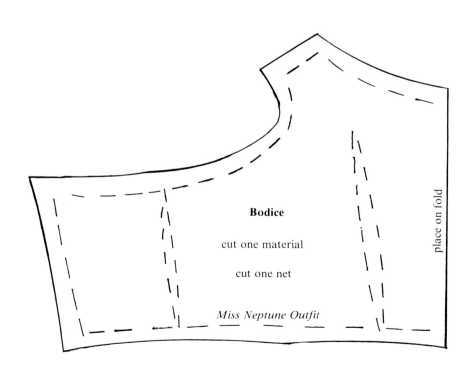

Bodice

cut one material

cut one net

Miss Neptune Outfit

place on fold

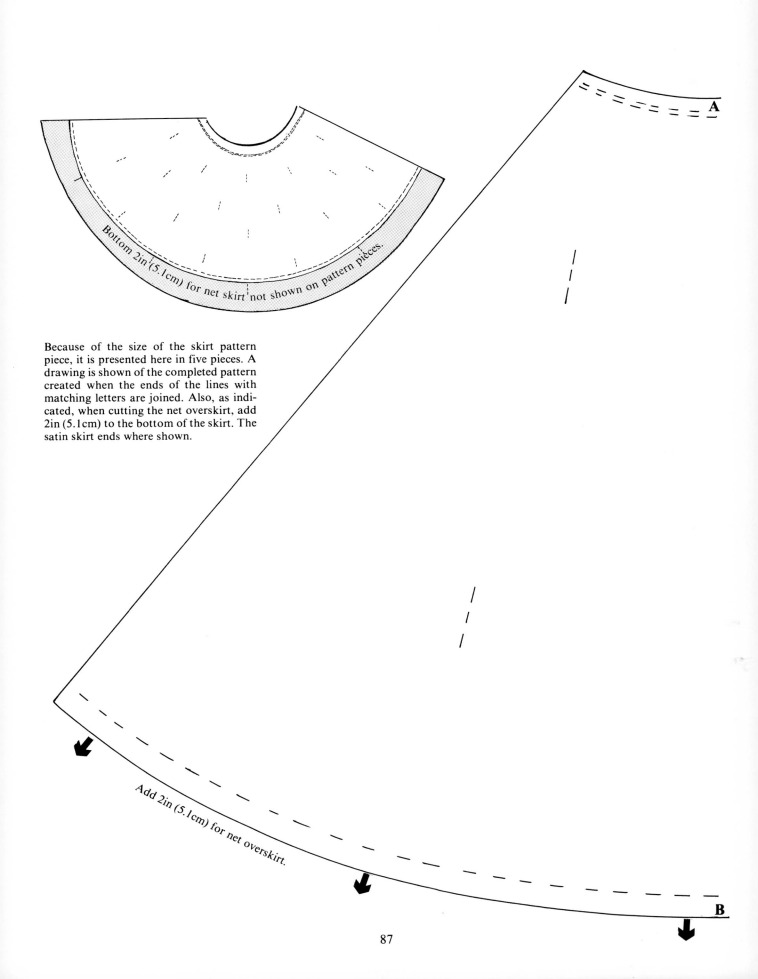

Because of the size of the skirt pattern piece, it is presented here in five pieces. A drawing is shown of the completed pattern created when the ends of the lines with matching letters are joined. Also, as indicated, when cutting the net overskirt, add 2in (5.1cm) to the bottom of the skirt. The satin skirt ends where shown.

Bottom 2in (5.1cm) for net skirt not shown on pattern pieces.

Add 2in (5.1cm) for net overskirt.

A

B

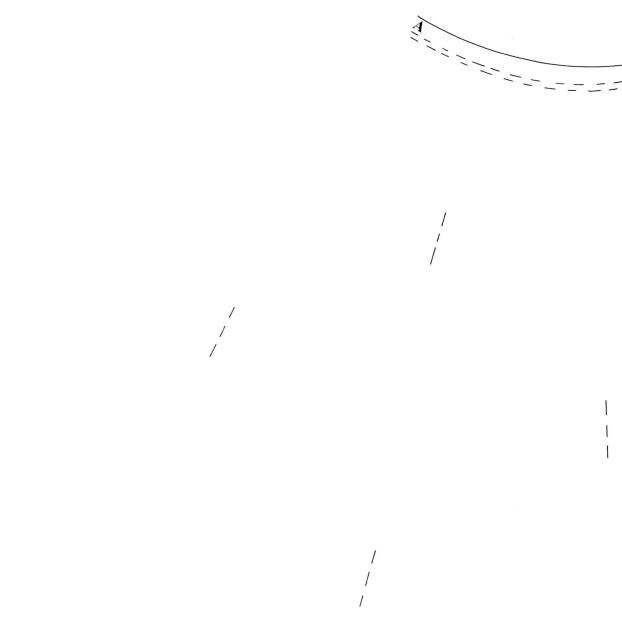

Add 2in (5.1cm) for net overskirt.

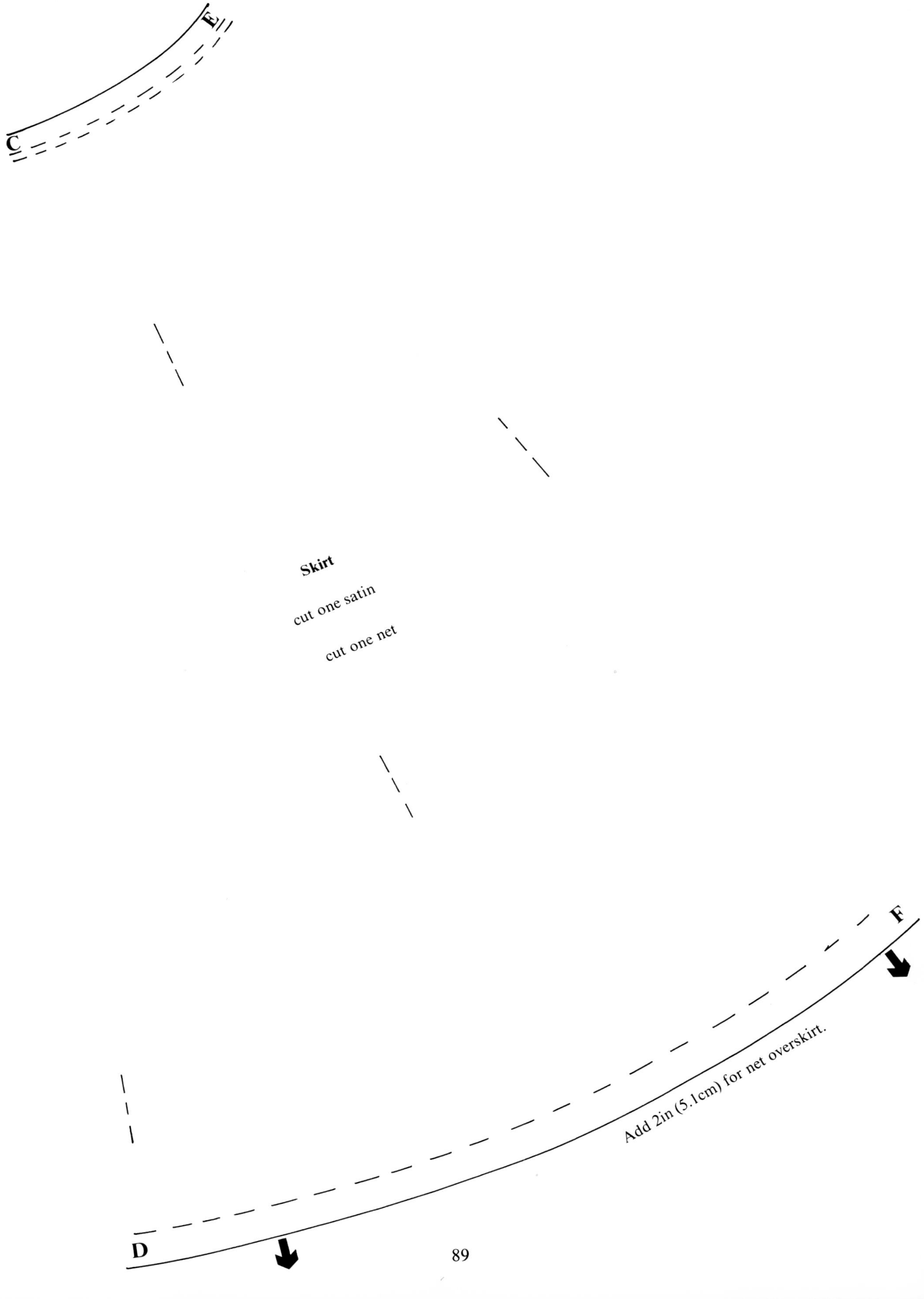

E

C

Skirt

cut one satin

cut one net

Add 2in (5.1cm) for net overskirt.

F

D

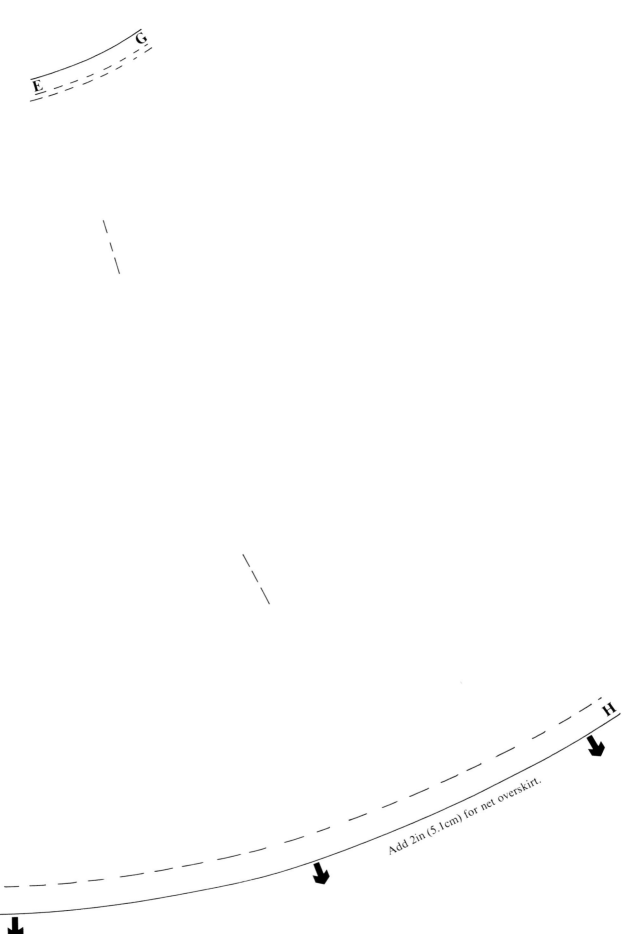

Add 2in (5.1cm) for net overskirt.

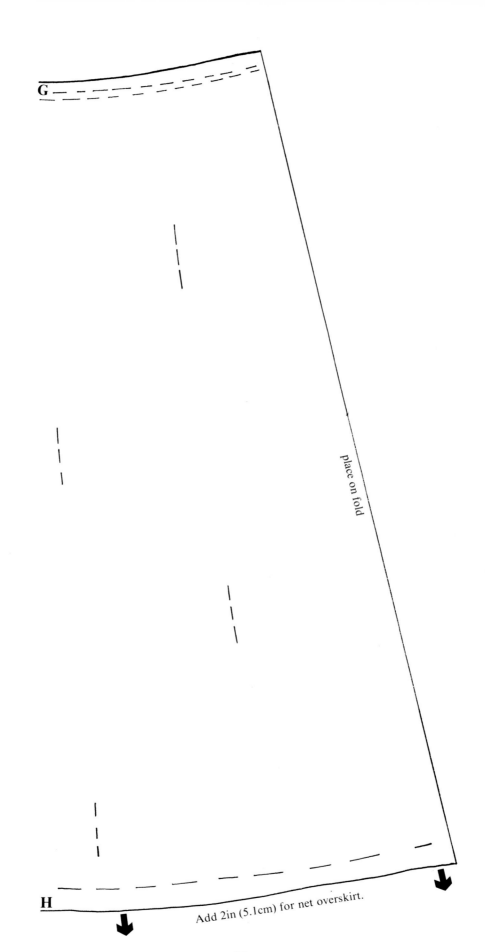

G

place on fold

H   Add 2in (5.1cm) for net overskirt.

Miss Pluto Outfit

Illustration 19. Miss Pluto. *Photograph by Scott Hime.*

Materials:

1/2yd (.46m) bridal satin
1/2yd (.46m) fine mesh nylon net
Fur: 2yd (1.82m) long, 7/8in (2.2cm)
 wide

See suggestions at end of instructions before purchasing fabric.

Be sure to measure garment on doll as you sew.

SATIN DRESS:

STRAPLESS BODICE: Lay net on right side of bodice and sew around backs and top of bodice. Clip edges and turn to right side. Sew darts as shown on pattern. Mark center of bodice.

SKIRT: Turn hem under and sew a double seam on bottom of skirt; sew vents at back. Mark center of skirt and gather to fit bodice. With right sides facing, sew skirt to bodice. Do not gather as much fullness at front of gown between darts of bodice. Be sure centers meet. Turn to right side and topstitch, turning raw edges toward bodice. Sew back of skirt together on wrong side.

NET COAT:

YOKE: Lay two pieces of net together and sew around neck edge and ends; clip edges, turn to right side. Now place markers with colored thread as follows: Measure 1¾in (4.5cm) from front edge, place marker (front). From this marker measure 1¾in (4.5cm), place another marker (sleeve); mark center back. Fold yoke in half and make two more markers for second front and sleeve at same place.

COAT: Lay fronts of net coat on back having raglan edges meet. Fold sleeves in half lengthwise and baste or pin raglan sleeve edges to fronts, then back of coat. Pin raw edges towards you; all raw edges will be on wrong side of coat. Mark center back of coat. When in place, sew raglan part of sleeves together. Now gather top edge of coat to measure same as bottom part of yoke. With right sides of coat facing yoke, sew coat to yoke having markers meeting at sleeve seams and center back. On right side of coat topstitch, turning raw edges toward yoke.

FUR: Sew fur around yoke, easing fur as you sew, making tiny pleats about 1/2in (1.3cm) apart. Slant fur a little wider at lower ends. Now sew fur on bottom of sleeves. Sew sleeve seams and side seams together on wrong side. Sew fur on bottom of coat about 3/4in (2cm) from bottom of coat.

FUR HEADDRESS: Fold 7½in (19.1cm) fur headdress in half and sew five small darts as shown on pattern.

NET: Sew two pieces of net together on top edge and ends; turn to right side. Now lay net on right side of fur and sew ends and bottom of fur together. Turn net to wrong side and sew net to top of leather edge, starting in center and ease net as you sew, if necessary.

FINISHING: Sew snaps on back of bodice and small snap at yoke opening on fur. Fasten headdress on head at ends of piece with pins or attach narrow elastic on ends to fit around back of head. Pins were used on the doll in the illustration.

SUGGESTIONS: Bridal satin was used for the outfit shown here but lighter weight satin can be used also if desired. The double sewing on the hem, about 1/2in (1.3cm) apart, gives the circular skirt a nice touch. The net can be firm or not too firm, but be sure it is a very fine mesh. Fit coat over doll dress on doll to ensure proper length when fur is sewn onto the coat. □

Reprinted from the August/September 1986 **Doll Reader**®.

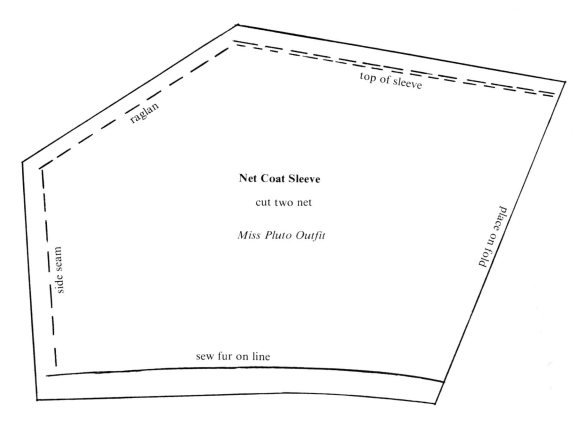

raglan

top of sleeve

side seam

Net Coat Sleeve

cut two net

Miss Pluto Outfit

place on fold

sew fur on line

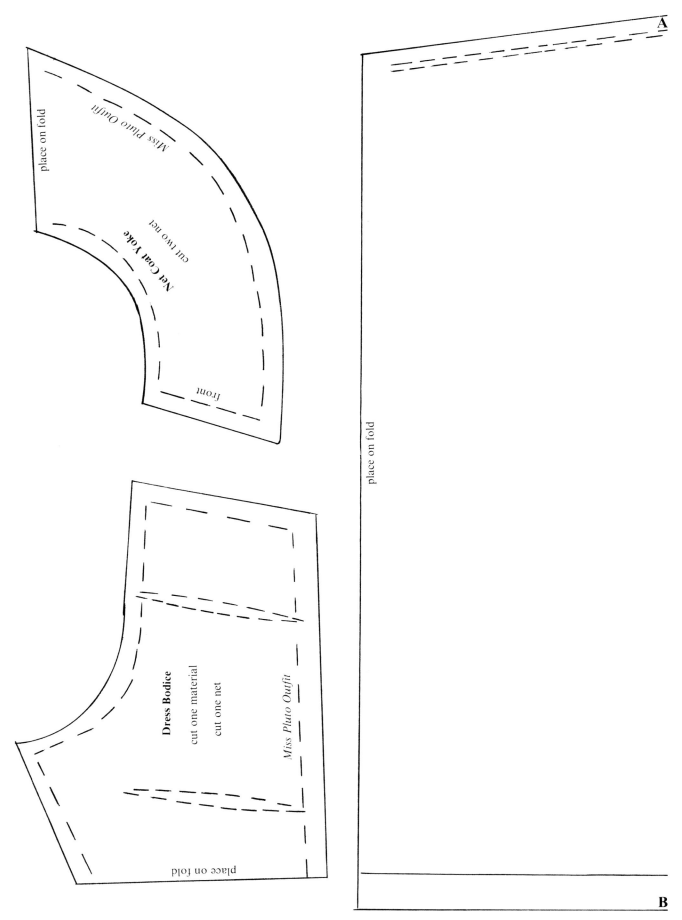

place on fold

Miss Pluto Outfit

Net Coat Yoke

cut two net

Front

Dress Bodice

cut one material

cut one net

Miss Pluto Outfit

place on fold

place on fold

A

place on fold

B

94

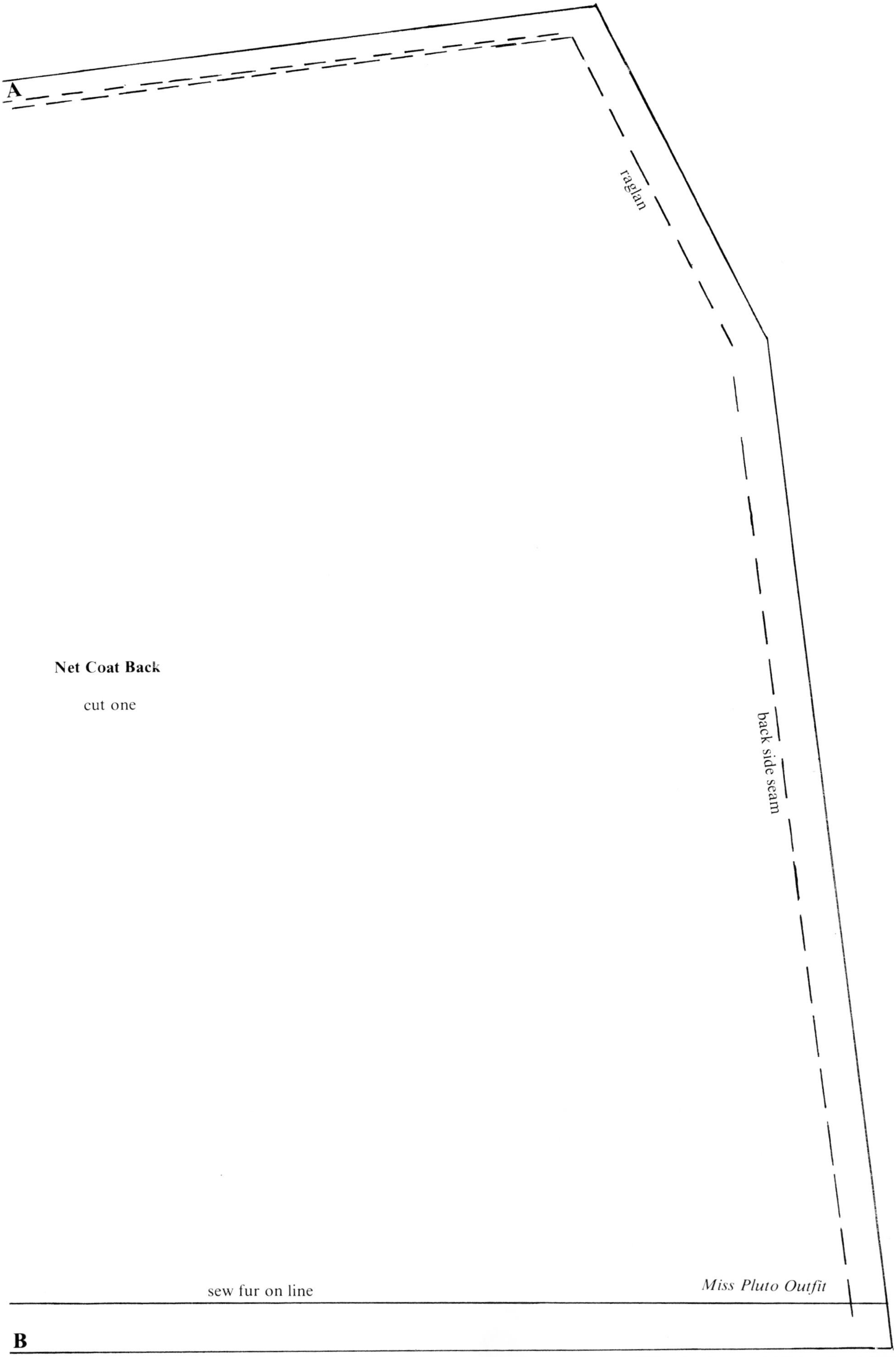

A

Net Coat Back

cut one

raglan

back side seam

sew fur on line

Miss Pluto Outfit

B

C

raglan

Miss Pluto Outfit

Net Coat Headdress

cut two

Net Lining

place on fold

front side seam

Net Coat Front

cut two

Miss Pluto Outfit

sew fur on line

D

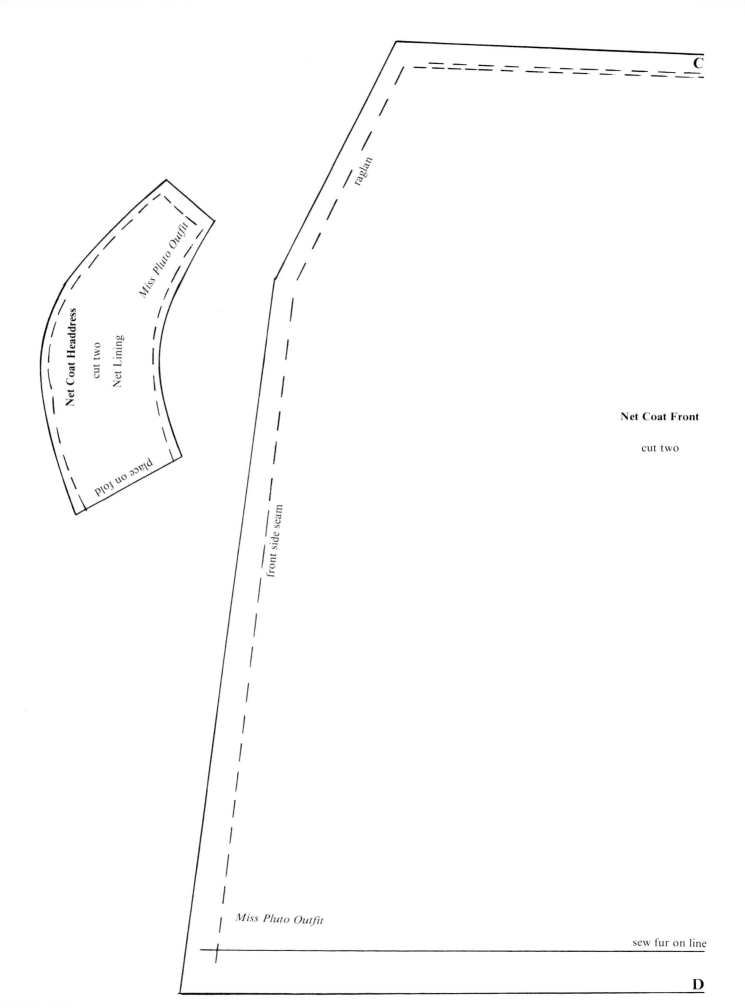

C

front

D

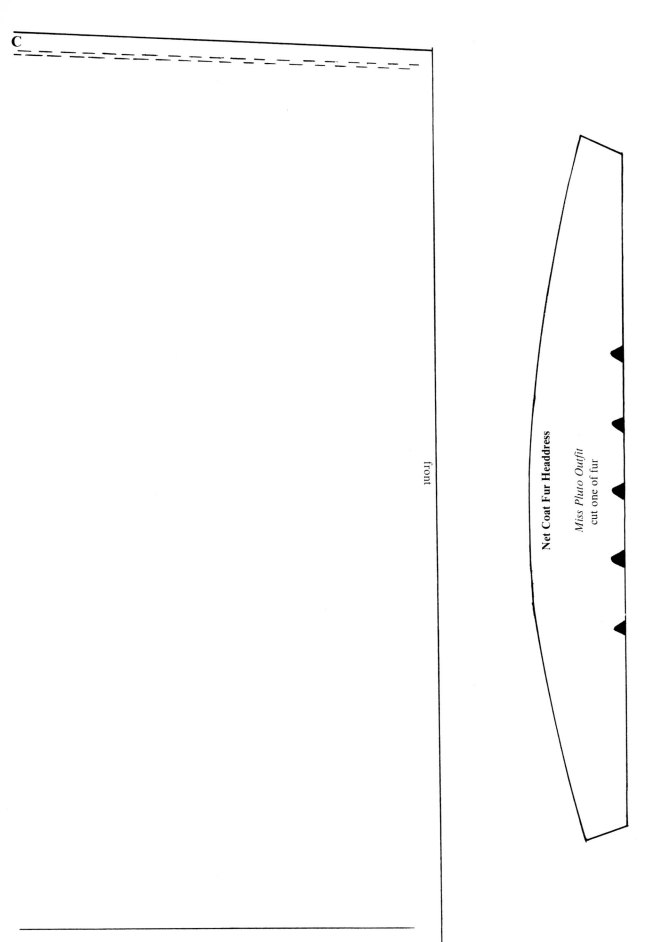

Net Coat Fur Headdress

Miss Pluto Outfit
cut one of fur

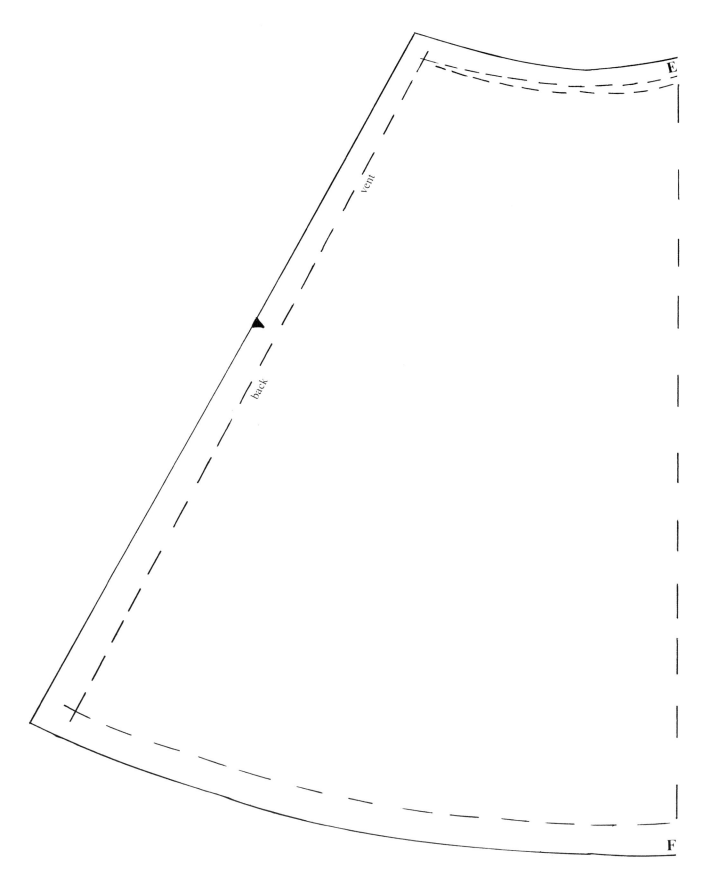

vent

back

E

F

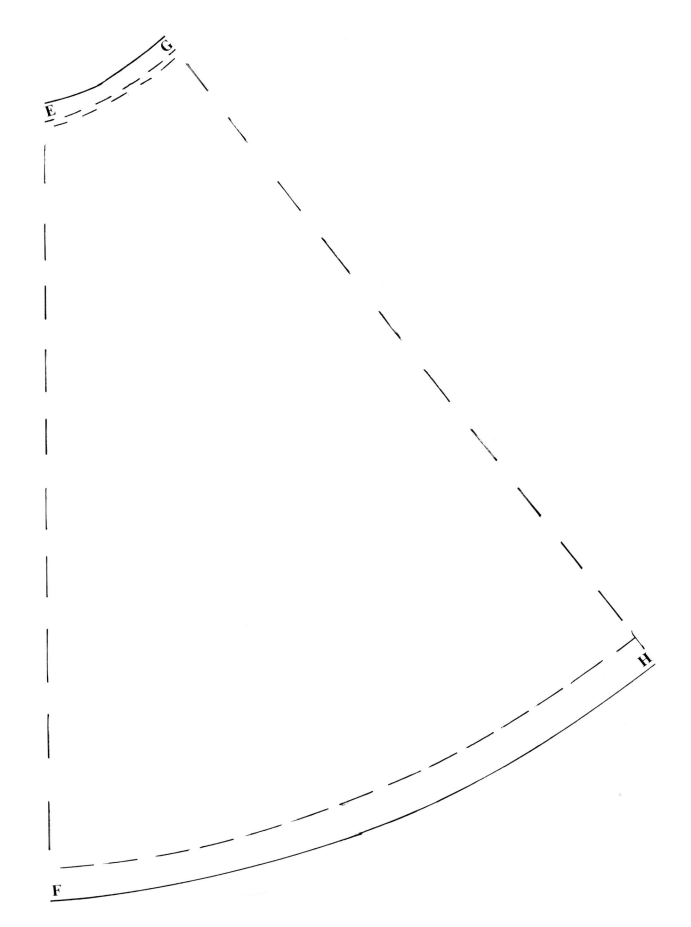

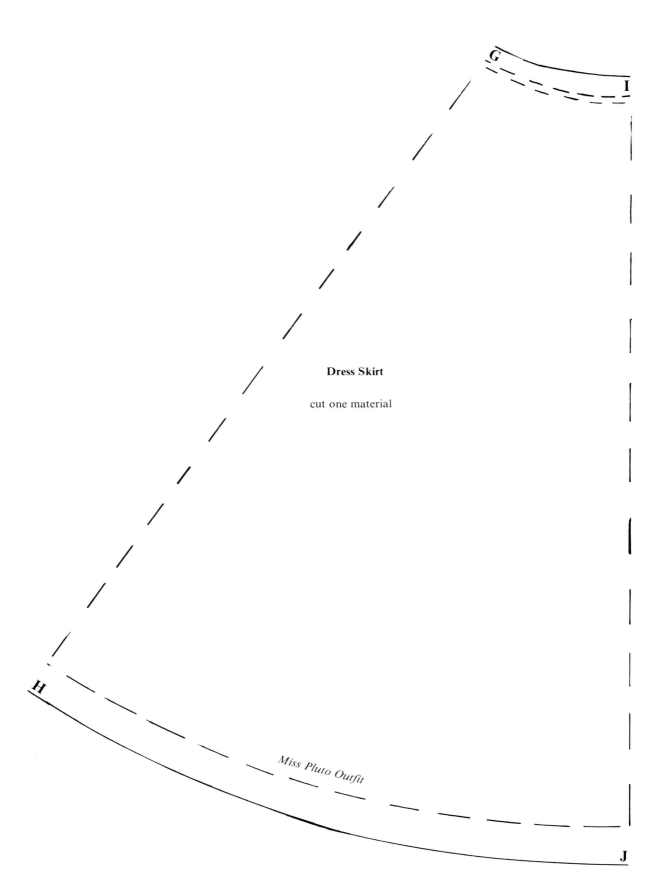

Dress Skirt

cut one material

Miss Pluto Outfit

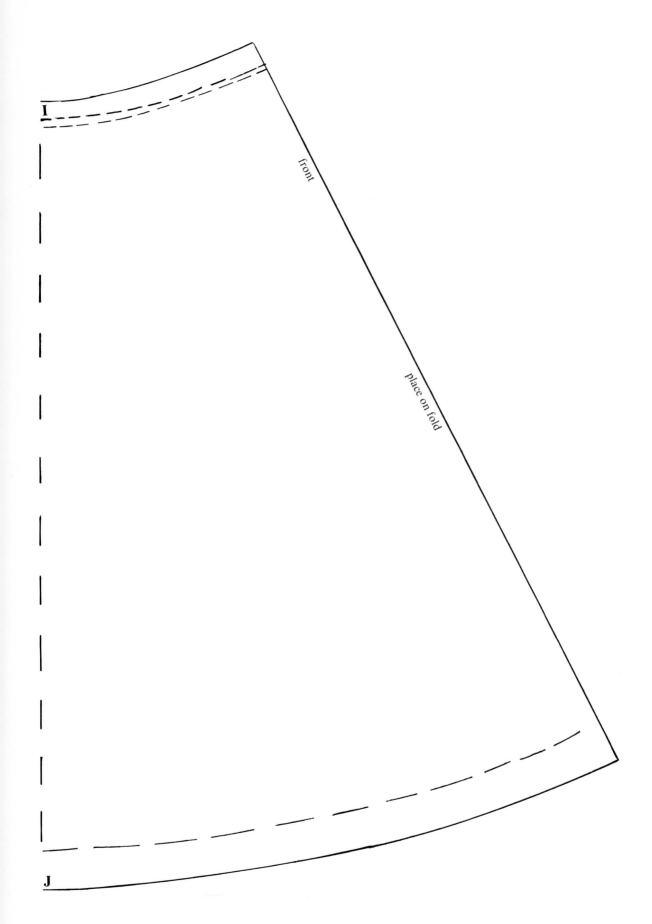

I

front

place on fold

J

Miss Mercury Outfit

Illustration 20. Miss Mercury. *Photograph by Scott Hime.*

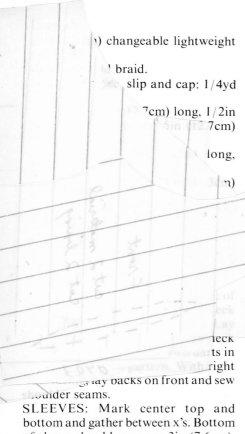

) changeable lightweight
' braid.
slip and cap: 1/4yd
7cm) long, 1/2in
5in (12.7cm)
long,
3 m)

neck

ts in

lay backs on front and sew
shoulder seams.

SLEEVES: Mark center top and
bottom and gather between x's. Bottom
of sleeve should measure 3in (7.6cm).

Hem bottom of lower piece of sleeve.
With right sides facing, sew top edge of
piece to lower edge of puffed sleeve
having most fullness across center part
of sleeve between x's. Sew braid on
sleeve as shown in illustration. Insert
sleeves into armholes, having most
fullness at top of sleeves.

SKIRT: Hem bottom of skirt and
mark center at top of skirt. From this
marker, place a marker 1/2in (1.3cm)
on either side. Hem vents at back and
gather skirt to measure same as bottom
of bodice. Do not gather skirt between
markers. With right sides facing, sew
skirt to bodice. Do not gather between
markers at center front. This should
come between darts on bodice.

SLIP: Hem bottom of slip and mark
center front at top. Gather slip to
measure 12in (30.5cm). Mark center of
elastic and sew elastic over gathers,
stretching elastic while sewing, having
markers meet. Sew back of slip.

PANTIES: Clip edges of legs as shown
on pattern and hem each leg. Now
gather lace over hem. With right sides
facing, fold piece in half and sew seam
on one side of panties. Mark center of
elastic and turn a hem over elastic and

sew across, stretching elastic as you
sew. Have center of elastic meet side
seam. Sew seam on open side of panties,
turn to right side.

JULIET CAP: Lay lining on right side
of four pieces of cap and sew bottom
edge. Turn to right side and press
lightly on wrong side. With right sides
facing, sew two pieces together from
bottom to top. Sew remaining two
pieces together in the same manner.
With right sides facing, lay pieces
together and sew across other half of
cap. Turn to right side and press seams
open on wrong side. On bottom of cap,
at center of one of the pieces, sew
braid, overlapping ends about 1/4in
(.65cm). Sew 1in (2.5cm) of braid into
a flat circle and sew on top of cap.

SUGGESTIONS: When purchasing
fabric for lining be sure the fabric has
firmness, especially the lining for the
cap. Match color as close as possible. □

Reprinted from the November 1987 **Doll
Reader** .

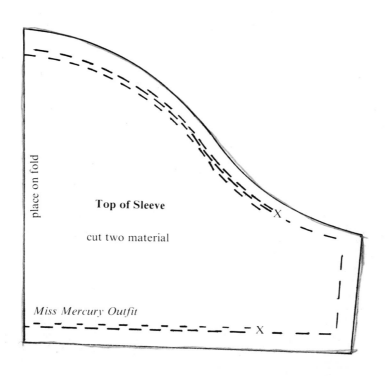

place on fold

Top of Sleeve

cut two material

X

Miss Mercury Outfit

X

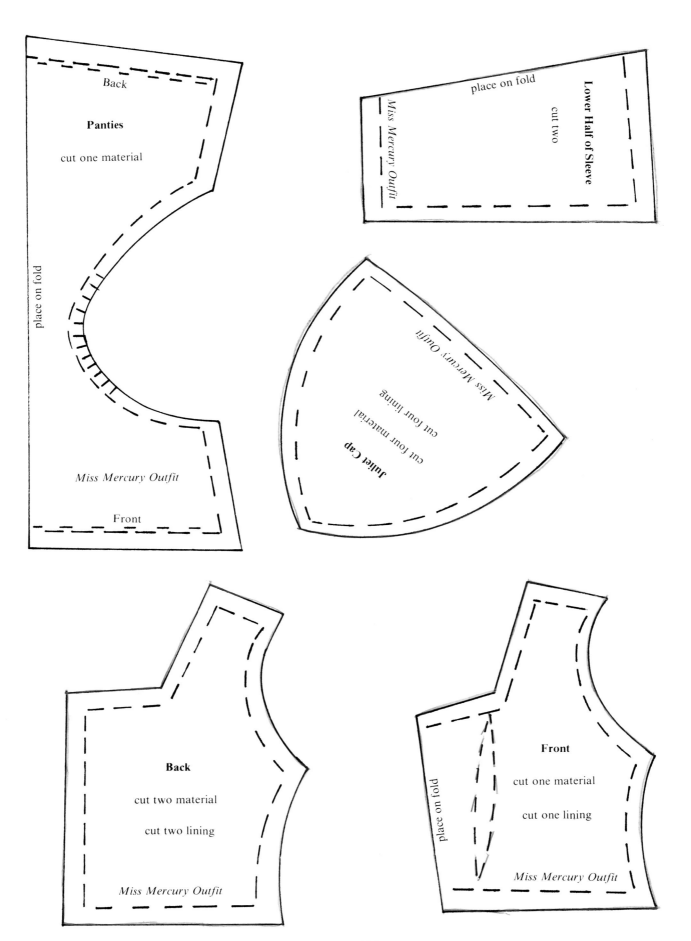

Back

Panties

cut one material

place on fold

Miss Mercury Outfit

Front

place on fold

Lower Half of Sleeve

cut two

Miss Mercury Outfit

Miss Mercury Outfit

Juliet Cap

cut four material
cut four lining

Back

cut two material

cut two lining

Miss Mercury Outfit

Front

cut one material

cut one lining

place on fold

Miss Mercury Outfit

Miss Venus Outfit

Illustration 21. Miss Venus. *Photograph by Clifford Yeich.*

Materials:

1yd (.91m) royal blue chiffon
1/3yd (.30m) light blue crepe
Silver bodice: 5in (12.7cm) long, 12in (30.5cm) wide
Bodice lining: 5in (12.7cm) long, 12in (30.5cm) wide
Elastic head band: 8in (20.3cm) long, 1/4in (.65cm) wide
Silver braid: 3½yd (3.18m) long, 1/4in (.65cm) wide
Chiffon skirt: 8¾in (22.3cm) long, 39in (99cm) wide
Crepe skirt: 8½in (21.6cm) long, 38in (96.5cm) wide

See suggestions before purchasing fabric.

Be sure to measure garment on doll as you sew.

BODICE: FRONT: Lay lining on right side of bodice and sew around neck edge and armholes, nip edges, turn to right side. Sew darts in front. BACKS: Lay lining on right side of backs and sew around neck edge and backs, nip edges, turn to right side. Sew small darts in backs. Lay right sides of backs to right side of front and sew shoulder seams.

CAPE: Mark front of cape and bottom on both pieces of cape (be sure fronts are facing). Sew vents at back of cape 5in (12.7cm) front top. Place marker 7in (17.8cm) from top of cape at fronts and measure 4in (10.2cm) from first marker and place another marker. Now turn back 1/4in (.65cm) on front and bottom and sew on silver braid; stretch crepe as much as possible between markers. This will drape better when point of front of cape is attached to shoulder. Gather top of cape to measure about 1¾in (4.5cm) to fit between shoulder seam and back, leave 1/8in (.31cm) from shoulder seam and 1/8in (.31cm) from edge at back. Now baste top of cape to back. Work second part of cape to correspond. Now attach points at bottom of cape at front and baste to shoulders. Sew braid around neck edge. Sew back seam.

SKIRT: Crepe: Hem bottom of skirt. Hem vents at back 4in (10.2cm) from top. SKIRT: Chiffon: Turn hem under 1/4in (.65cm) and sew on braid. Hem vents at back 4in (10.2cm) from top. Mark center of bodice and center of both skirts separately. Lay chiffon skirt on right side of crepe skirt having centers of skirts meet. Now gather skirts together to fit bodice having centers meet. Ease chiffon at back and sides. With right sides facing, sew skirts to bodice having centers of skirts meet with center of bodice. Turn to right side and topstitch.

FINISHING: Sew back of cape to vent. Sew skirts together separately. Sew two snaps on bodice.

HEAD BAND: Sew two rows of silver braid on elastic, stretching slightly while sewing. Sew ends together.

SUGGESTIONS: Chiffon and light-weight crepe fabric were used in the gown shown. However, lightweight taffeta and soft net can be used very effectively. These materials are easier to work with than chiffon and crepe. □

Reprinted from the October 1985 **Doll Reader**®.

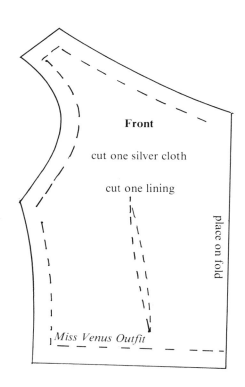

Front

cut one silver cloth

cut one lining

place on fold

Miss Venus Outfit

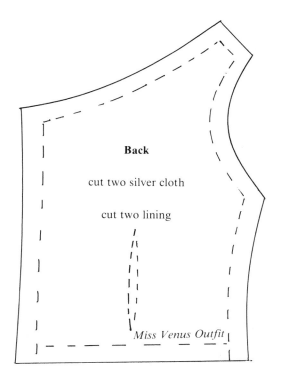

Back

cut two silver cloth

cut two lining

Miss Venus Outfit

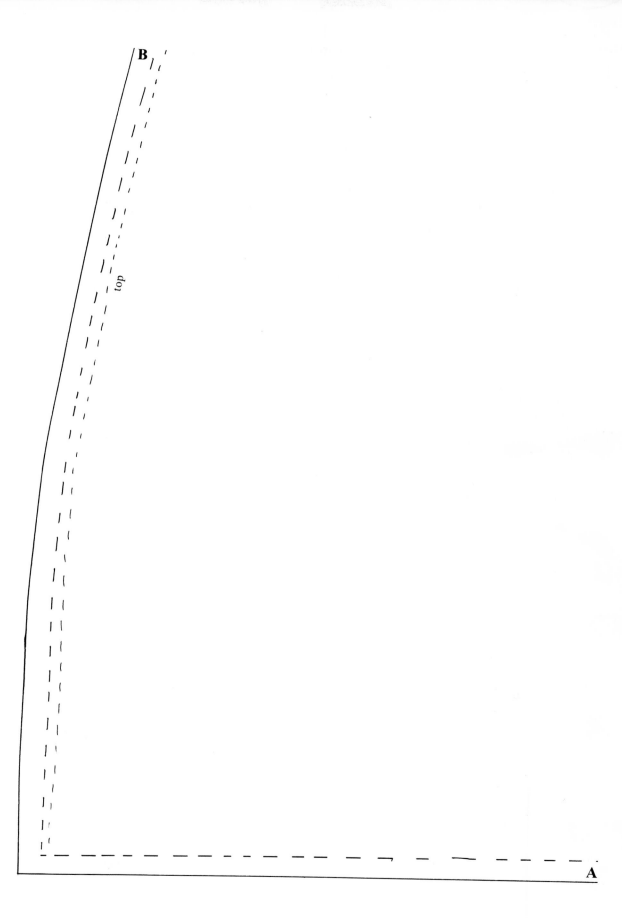

top

B

A

C

bottom

Cape

cut two chiffon

A

front

Miss Venus Outfit

108

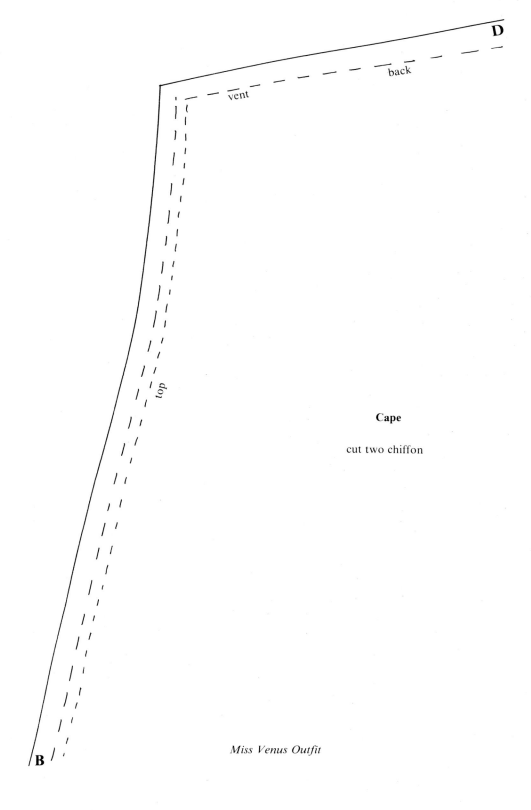

D

vent

back

top

Cape

cut two chiffon

Miss Venus Outfit

B

Miss Earth Outfit

Illustration 22. Miss Earth. *Photograph by Scott Hime.*

Materials:

Bodice: gold or silver lamé

Skirt: 1/4yd (.23m) chiffon

Lining — bodice and slip: 1/4yd (.23m) lightweight crepe or lining

Lame: 6in (15.2cm) long, 12in (30.5cm) wide

Skirt: 6½in (15.9cm) long, 40in (101.6cm) wide

Lining: 6¼in (15.9cm) long, 40in (101.6cm) wide

Sash: 10¼in (26.1cm) long, 2¼in (5.8cm) wide

Ties on shoulder and hip: 14in (35.6cm) long, 2¼in (5.8cm) wide, cut two pieces

See suggestions at end of instructions before purchasing fabric.

Be sure to measure garment on doll as you sew.

BODICE: Lay lining on right side of front, sew around neck edge and armhole, clip edges, turn to right side. Sew darts as shown on pattern. Lay lining on right side of back (with one armhole), and sew across top, back and armhole. Clip edges and turn to right side. On other half of back, lay lining on right side and sew across top and back, turn to right. Sew darts on back as shown on pattern. With right sides facing, lay backs on front and sew shoulder seam and side seams. Sew across bottom edge of bodice and measure 1/2in (1.3cm) above this edge and sew across. This will be a guideline when sewing on skirt.

CHIFFON SKIRT: Fold skirt in half and mark top and bottom with contrasting thread. Fold both ends of skirt to meet markers at center. Place markers on fold at each end of skirt. Now pin across top of piece and turn skirt to other side. Opening ends will be back of skirt. Lay finished bodice at top of skirt. On the long side of bodice, cut skirt on this half as follows: Measure 3/4in (2cm) at folded end to center marking, place ruler and mark a line. Cut slanting piece on line. This shorter side of skirt will fit the longer side of bodice (see illustration). Now mark hem so it will be on the proper side of dress when finished.

LINING: Work lining skirt in same manner as chiffon skirt. Place markers exactly as on chiffon. Sew vents at back and hem bottom of skirts separately. Lay chiffon skirt over lining, having markers meet. Be sure lining hem does not show below chiffon hem. Now gather skirts to fit bodice. With right side of skirts towards you, lay on right side of bodice (raw edge will be covered with sash), baste together, then sew. Use guideline for the top of skirt. Sew back of skirts together separately.

SASH: Press about 1/2in (1.3cm) pleat in center of band, lengthwise. Pleat will turn toward bodice (right side). Sew edge of band on seam, leaving 1/2in (1.3cm) on each end to turn under. Turn to right side, turn edge under and sew top of band and ends. Sew tie on sash at hip and shoulder as follows: Fold piece in half lengthwise and sew together, sloping ends. Attach narrow ribbon on end before sewing, then pull piece through to right side and press. Sew second end by hand. Attach bow on hip and shoulder as follows: Rip a few stitches from side seam at hip on top and bottom of sash. Slip sash through opening and tie a bow. Tie bow directly on shoulder. Sew four small snaps at back.

SUGGESTIONS: If your bodice fabric is very sheer, you can use lining a little firmer or heavier than the skirt lining. Lightweight taffeta was used for the gown in the illustration.

Make a marker with contrasting thread for exact placing of darts before sewing.

Bows can be made separately and sewn in place if desired. □

Reprinted from the October 1986 **Doll Reader**®.

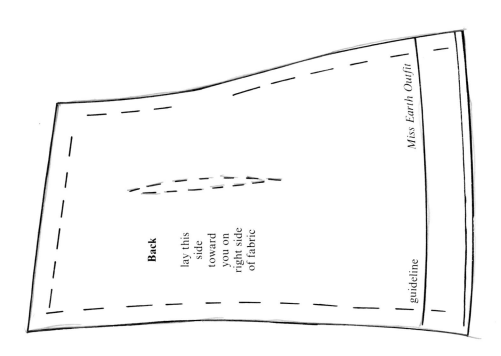

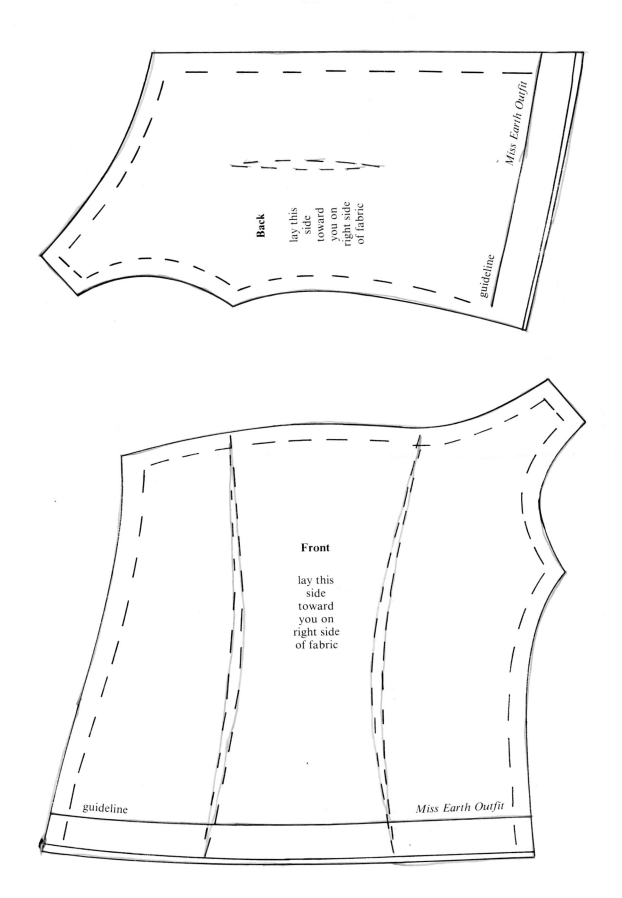

Back

lay this side toward you on right side of fabric

guideline

Miss Earth Outfit

Front

lay this
side
toward
you on
right side
of fabric

guideline

Miss Earth Outfit

Holiday Ensemble

Illustration 23. Coat, hat and muff from the Holiday Ensemble. *Photograph by Scott Hime.*

Materials:

Coat and Bonnet: 1/2yd (.46m) red velvet

Lining: 12in (30.5cm) long, 16in (40.6cm) wide lightweight red taffeta for collar and bonnet

Collar: 12in (30.5cm) long, 1/2in (1.3cm) wide white fur

Bonnet Brim: 11½in (29.2cm) long, 1in (2.5cm) wide white fur

Dress: 1/4yd (.23m) white skinner satin

Gauntlets: 8in (20.3cm) long, 5in (12.7cm) wide spandex

Muff: two pieces 4in (10.2cm) long, 3/4in (2cm) wide white fur

Ribbon for Muff: 7in (17.8cm) long, 1/4in (.65cm) wide white satin

25in (63.5cm) long, 1/4in (.65cm) wide seam tape

See suggestions before purchasing fabric.

Be sure to measure garment on doll as you sew.

NOTE: Cut all velvet pieces of pattern with the nap running upwards.

DRESS: FRONT: With right sides facing, baste (or sew with large stitches) side panels to front. BACK: Lay right sides of backs on right side of front and baste side seams in same manner. Sew small darts in back. Baste vents at back. Now try dress on doll and adjust seams to fit body. The top edge of dress will be about 1/2in (1.3cm) below the underarms. (This will fit when sewing red velvet bias piece on dress.) Sew all seams and vents, take out bastings. Clip edges at waistline and press seams open on wrong side. With right sides facing, sew bias red velvet piece on edge at top of dress, leaving 1/2in (1.3cm) ends to turn under. Ease velvet as you sew, easing center front panel as much as possible (do not gather). Now turn band under and topstitch. When sewing velvet on right side be sure stitching does not show on velvet. Hem dress and sew back of skirt together.

Fasten dress with three small snaps.

GAUNTLETS: Sew hem at top of gauntlets as shown on pattern. Fold piece in half on wrong side and make a narrow seam. Now tailor tack top and bottom of seam, turn to right side. Stretch gauntlet on doll's arm and stitch securely between thumb and fingers. Make second gauntlet in same manner.

COAT: FRONT: On both fronts of coat, baste darts as shown on pattern (to be adjusted later). BACK: With right sides facing, sew side panels to center back panel, starting at top of coat. Lay right side of fronts on right side of back and sew shoulder seams.

SLEEVES: Hem bottom of sleeve and sew darts. Mark center of sleeve at top and insert sleeve into armhole. Make small pleats at top of sleeve. Starting at bottom of sleeve, sew sleeve seams and side seams of coat. Clip curved edges.

COLLAR: Lay lining on right side of velvet and sew around ends and outside of collar (sew seam close to edge), turn to right side. Press seams of coat and collar lightly on wrong side. Mark center of collar and center of coat at neck edge. Lay wrong side of collar on right side of coat and baste to neck edge, starting at center back. Ends of collar should come within 1/4in (.65cm) from front of coat on fold (see line on pattern). Now turn back front fold on right side of coat (over collar) and baste. Work other side of collar in same manner; now sew together. Turn coat to right side. You should have 1/4in (.65cm) extension from collar for closing. Now sew seam tape on raw seams at neck edge. Turn binding on wrong side of coat and stitch by hand. On bottom of coat, fold back on line and sew (same as top of coat), turn to right side. Now sew tape on bottom of

Illustration 24. Dress with gauntlets from the Holiday Ensemble. *Photograph by Scott Hime.*

coat on right side, turn tape on wrong side and stitch by hand.

Sew fronts on fold by hand and adjust darts after fitting coat over dress and machine-stitch. Sew two snaps on front.

BONNET: BACK: Lay wrong side of lining on wrong side of velvet, pin or baste in place. With right sides facing, sew back together. Turn to right side, press seams open. On velvet edge at front, turn under 1/4in (.65cm) hem and baste. Turn lining in same manner toward velvet, and baste.

BRIM: Lay right sides together, sew around outer edge and ends, turn to right side. Now sew raw edges together on right side. Mark center of brim and center front of bonnet. Insert brim between lining and velvet. Ends of brim should be about 1/4in (.65cm) shorter on each end at back of bonnet. Starting at center on velvet side of bonnet, baste brim (not lining) across front; when in place, sew. Turn under hem at back of bonnet. Now topstitch and overwhip raw edges.

FUR TRIM: Mark center of brim and center of top edge of fur. Starting at center of front of brim and center of fur piece, hand-stitch edge of fur to edge of brim. Taper ends of fur to fit brim. Now sew other end of brim. On front edge of fur, machine-stitch or hand-stitch bottom of fur, making tiny darts as needed to fit brim. Baste hem at bottom of bonnet and topstitch (over-whip raw edges).

MUFF: FUR: On right side of fur, sew two 4in (10.2cm) pieces together on edge at center. Now sew satin ribbon on each side of ribbon over center seam. Hem lining on each side as shown on pattern. Lining should measure same as fur on wrong side. Turn fur piece on wrong side and sew ends together; turn to right side. Sew ends together on lining on wrong side. Press seams open and insert into muff. Sew ends of lining to end of fur. Attach ribbon (to loop over hand) on side at top of muff.

SUGGESTIONS: The coat and bonnet were made of imported washable cotton velvet made in China. It is very light-weight and easy to sew. When cutting velvet, cut all pieces with the nap running upwards.

Lace was used for binding instead of tape in this coat.

The fur that was used is real rabbit fur, cut in strips. Lightweight imitation fur can be used if real fur cannot be obtained. If using imitation fur, the ends of the fabric may not extend beyond the skin like real fur and you may want to cut the fabric a little wider to appear the same as real fur. Also you may not need a lining.

Ties may be worn on the bonnet with narrow white velvet ribbons if desired.

The fur on the front of the brim may be machine-stitched or sewn by hand. □

Reprinted from the December 1985/January 1986 **Doll Reader***.

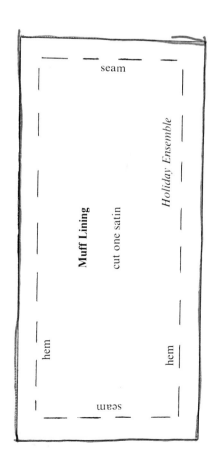

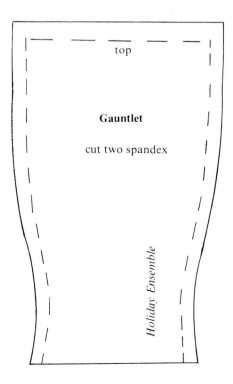

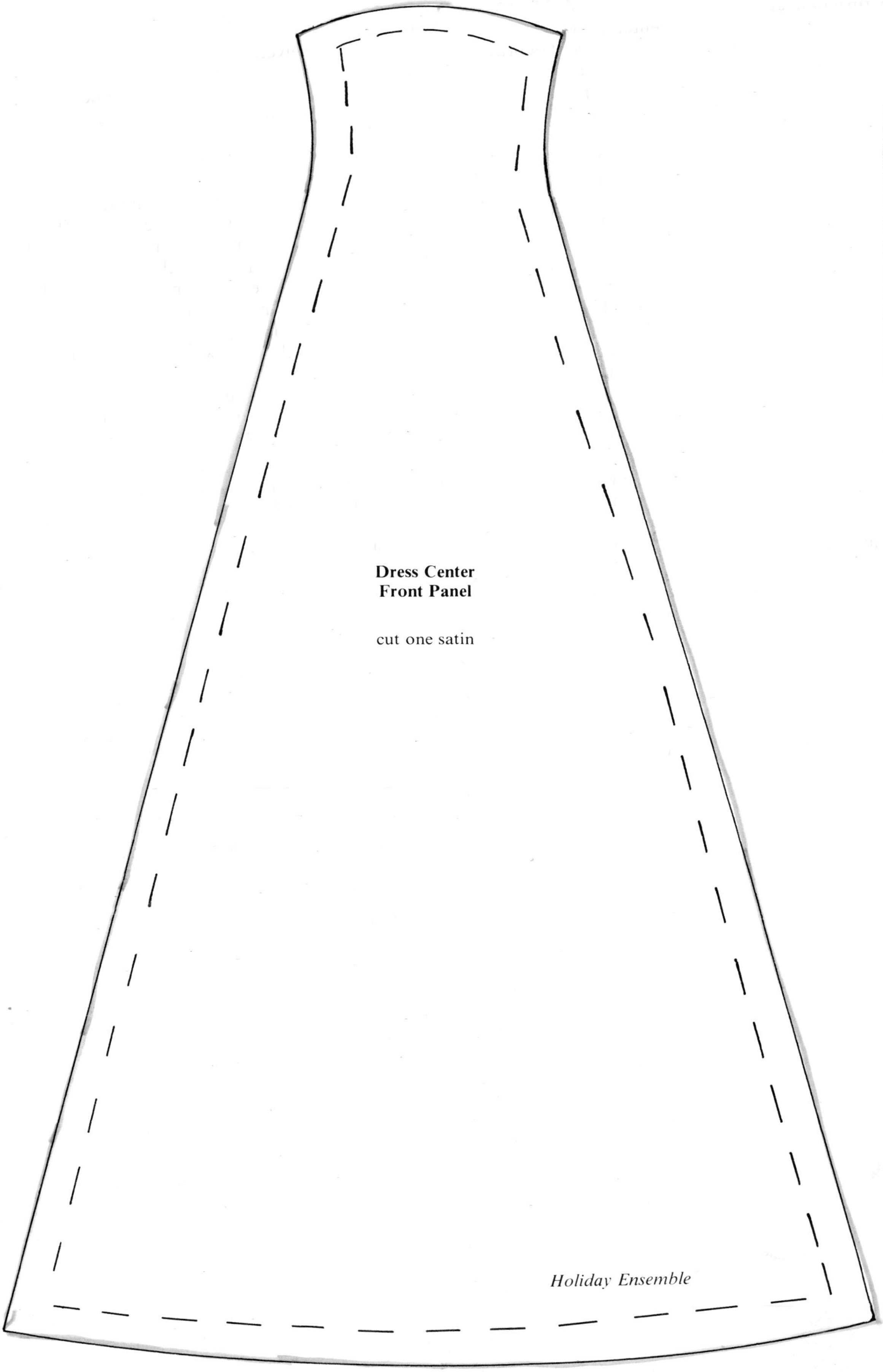

**Dress Center
Front Panel**

cut one satin

Holiday Ensemble

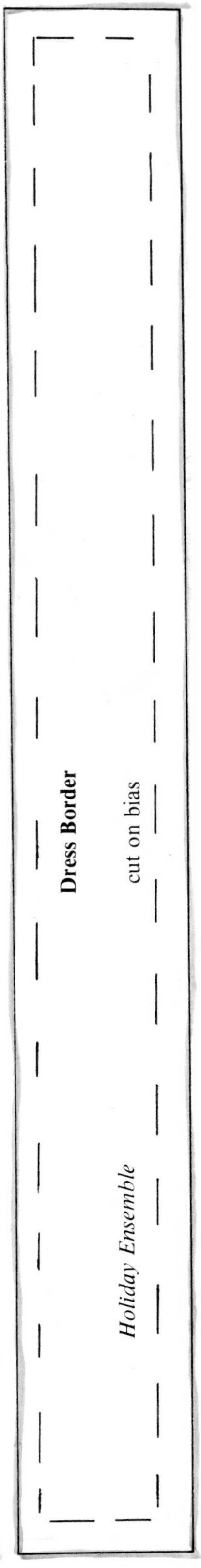

Dress Border

cut on bias

Holiday Ensemble

117

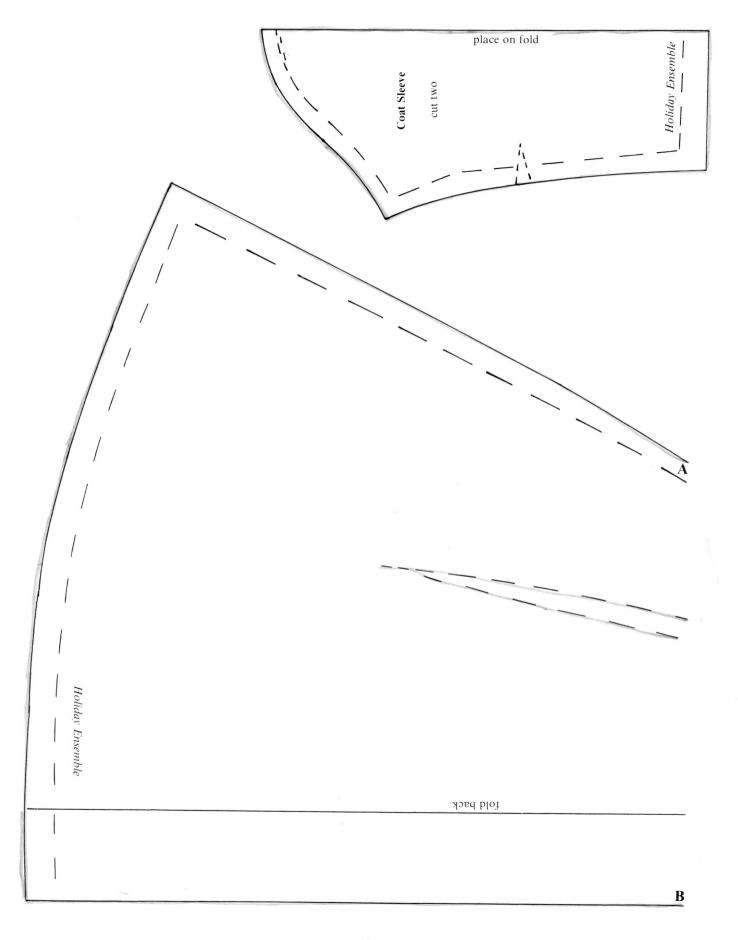

place on fold

Coat Sleeve

cut two

Holiday Ensemble

A

Holiday Ensemble

fold back

B

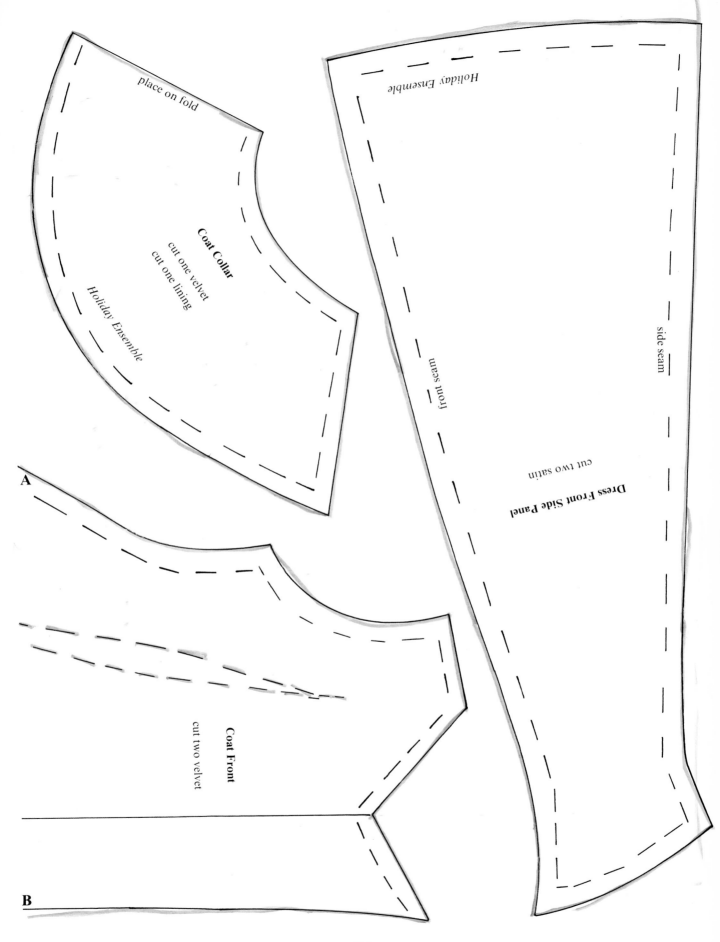

place on fold

Coat Collar

cut one velvet
cut one lining

Holiday Ensemble

Holiday Ensemble

front seam

side seam

cut two satin

Dress Front Side Panel

A

Coat Front

cut two velvet

B

119

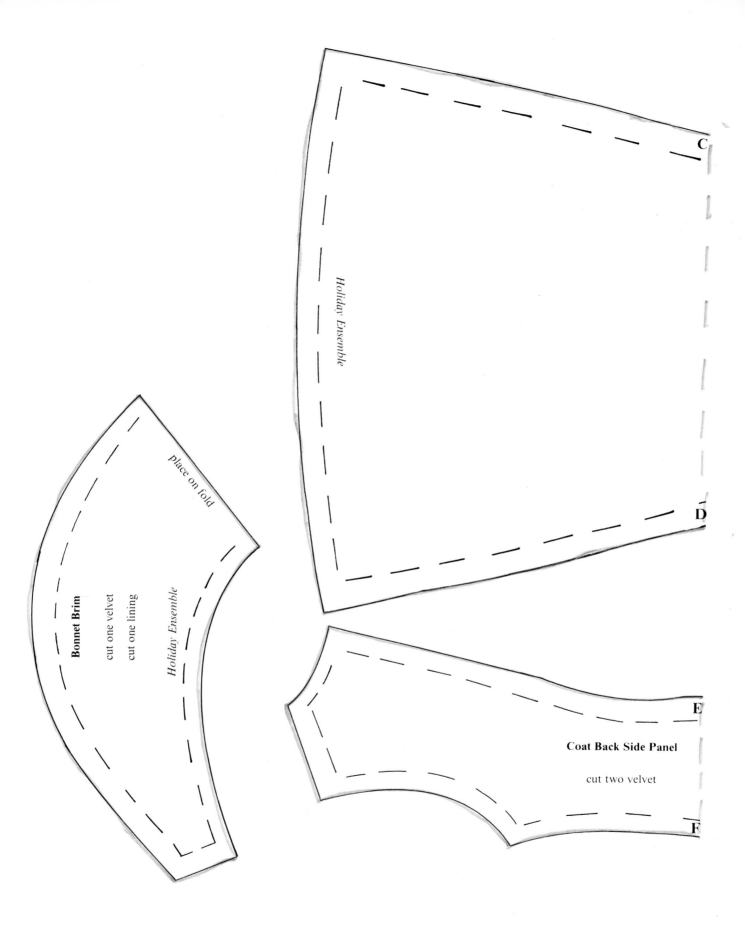

Holiday Ensemble

C

D

Bonnet Brim

cut one velvet

cut one lining

place on fold

Holiday Ensemble

E

Coat Back Side Panel

cut two velvet

F

120

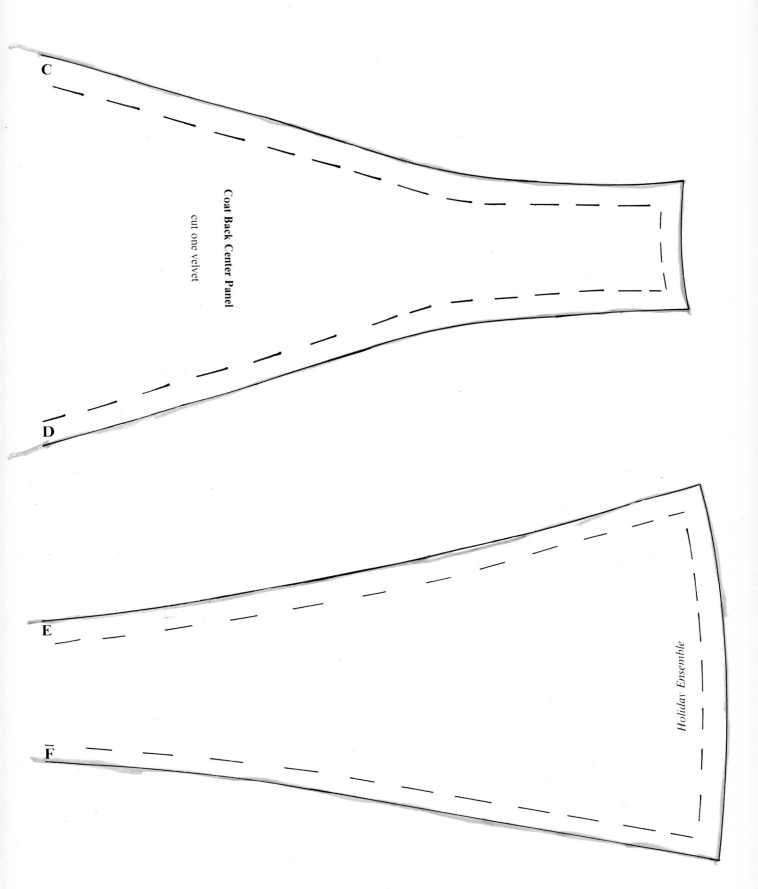

C

Coat Back Center Panel

cut one velvet

D

E

Holiday Ensemble

F

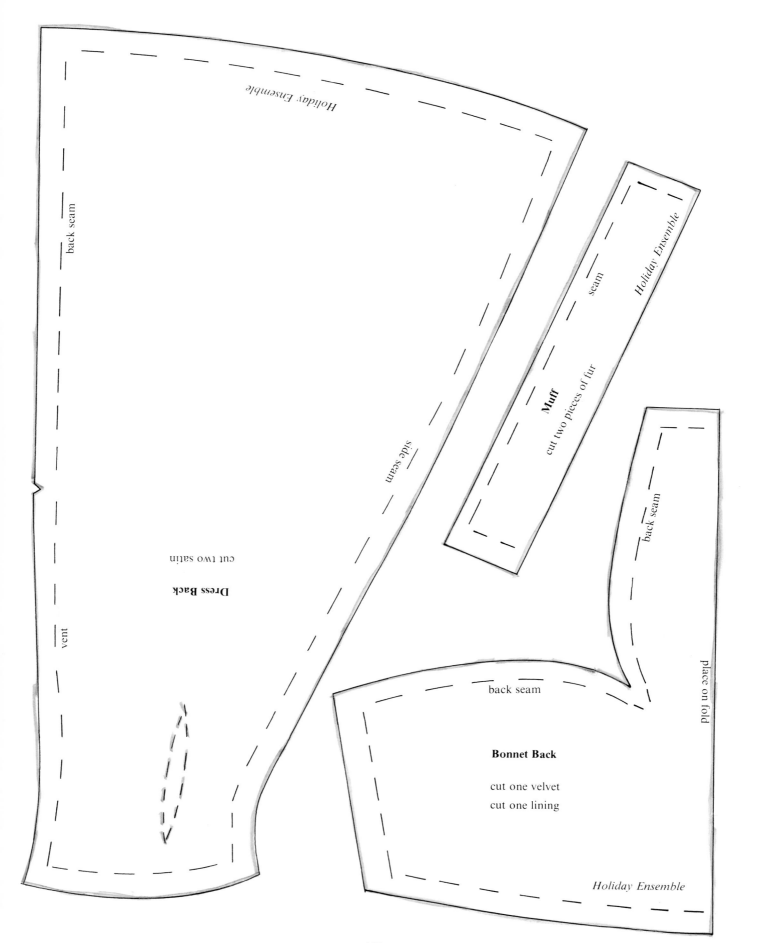

back seam

Holiday Ensemble

vent

cut two satin

Dress Back

side seam

Muff

cut two pieces of fur

seam

Holiday Ensemble

back seam

place on fold

back seam

Bonnet Back

cut one velvet

cut one lining

Holiday Ensemble

Nightie and Peignoir

Illustration 25. Peignoir and nightie. *Photograph by Scott Hime.*

Illustration 26. Peignoir. *Photograph by Scott Hime.*

Illustration 27. Nightie. *Photograph by Scott Hime.*

Materials:
Nightie: 1/4yd (.23m) lightweight cotton, plain color
Peignoir: 1/2yd (.46m) lightweight flowered cotton
3yd (2.73m) of 1in (2.5cm) lace
2½yd (2.28m) of 1/4in (.65cm) ribbon
Nightie: 7½in (19.1cm) long, 27in (68.6cm) wide
Sleeve bands: 3in (7.6cm) long, 1in (2.5cm) wide

Be sure to measure garment on doll as you sew.
NIGHTIE: FRONTS: With right sides facing, lay two pieces of fronts together and sew around front and armholes. Clip edges and turn to right side. Sew darts in front as shown in pattern. Sew other half of front in same manner. Now sew backs together in same manner. Place fronts together overlapping 1/2in (1.3cm) at center front, baste together at bottom of overlap. Lay front and backs together and sew shoulder seams and side seams. Try on doll and adjust front to fit waistline, leaving 1/2in (1.3cm) overlap for back closing.
SKIRT: Turn under 1/4in (.65cm) on

wrong side of skirt at bottom and sew on lace, stretching material as you sew on lace. Sew vents at back and mark center top of skirt. Now gather skirt to measure same as waist on nightie. With right sides facing, sew skirt to bodice (do not have too much fullness in center of front). Turn to right side and topstitch.
SASH: Measure 26in (66cm) of ribbon and fold in half. Sew ribbon on seam at waistline, having fold at center. Sew ribbon to within 1/2in (1.3cm) on either end of back. Sew on snap. Tie bow at back.
PEIGNOIR: YOKE: With right sides facing, lay two pieces of yoke together and sew around neck edge and ends. Clip edges and turn to right side. Now place markers with colored thread as follows: Measure 1¾in (4.5cm) from edge, place marker (front). From this marker, measure 1¾in (4.5cm), place another marker (sleeve). Mark center back. Fold yoke in half and make two more markers for second front and sleeve at same place. With right sides facing, lay fronts on back. Now fold sleeves in half lengthwise and baste or pin raglan sleeve edges to fronts, then back of peignoir. Pin raw edges toward you; all raw edges will be on wrong side

of pieces. Mark center back. When in place, sew raglan sleeve to back and fronts. Press seams open. Turn front edges back 1/2in (1.3cm) and sew. Now gather fronts, sleeves and back together to measure same as bottom of yoke. With right sides facing, sew gathered piece to yoke, having markers meet raglan seams and center back. Topstitch on right side, turning edges toward yoke. Gather lace over seam on yoke, fold ends under 1/4in (.65cm) at beginning and end of lace. Be sure gathers are full. Now gather bottom of sleeves to measure 3in (7.6cm) and sew bands on as follows: With right sides facing, sew band over gathers, and topstitch on wrong side. Sew sleeve seams and side seams together. Now turn hem under and sew on lace. Stretch hem as you sew on lace. Sew ribbon over lace, turn ends under fronts. Fold 32in (81.3cm) of ribbon in half and place marker. Start sewing ribbon 1/2in (1.3cm) from end of yoke over edge of gathered lace, having markers at center back. Tie ends of ribbon as shown in illustration. Sew snap at front of bottom of yoke. □

Reprinted from the February/March 1987 **Doll Reader**.

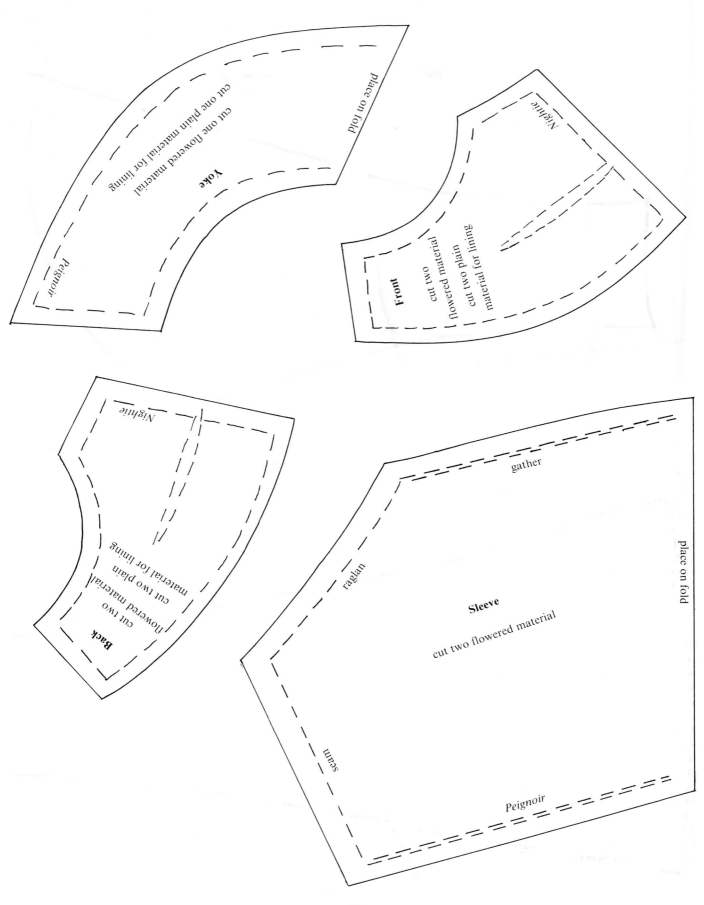

Yoke

cut one flowered material
cut one plain material for lining

Peignoir

place on fold

Front

Nightie

cut two
flowered material
cut two plain
material for lining

Back

Nightie

cut two
flowered material
cut two plain
material for lining

Peignoir

Sleeve

cut two flowered material

gather

raglan

seam

place on fold

Peignoir

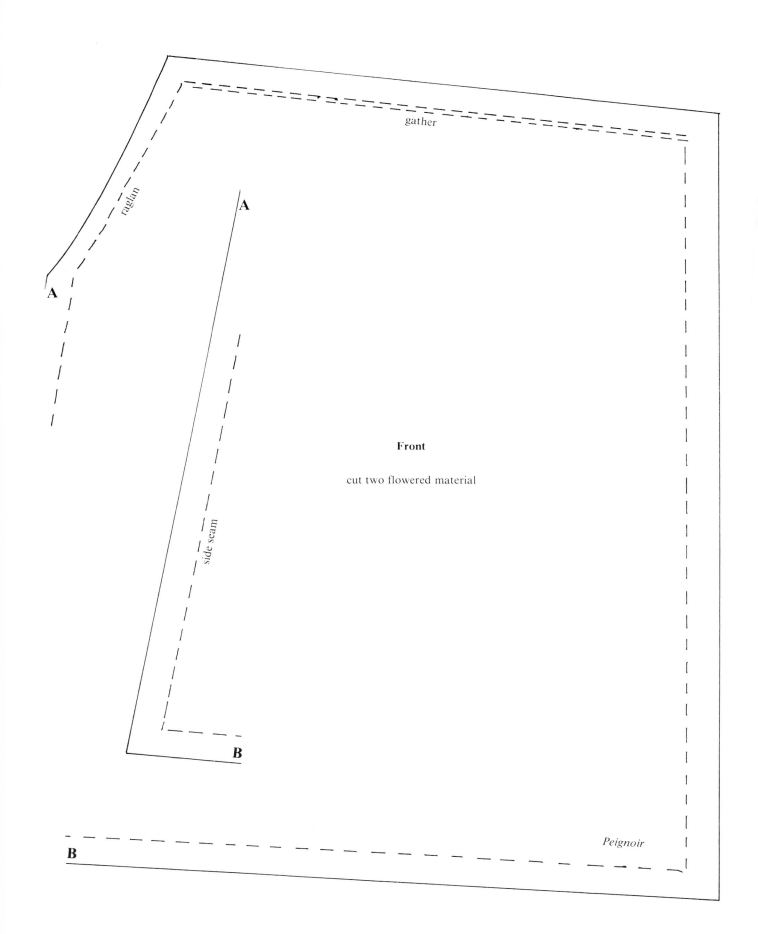

gather

raglan

A

A

side seam

Front

cut two flowered material

B

B

Peignoir

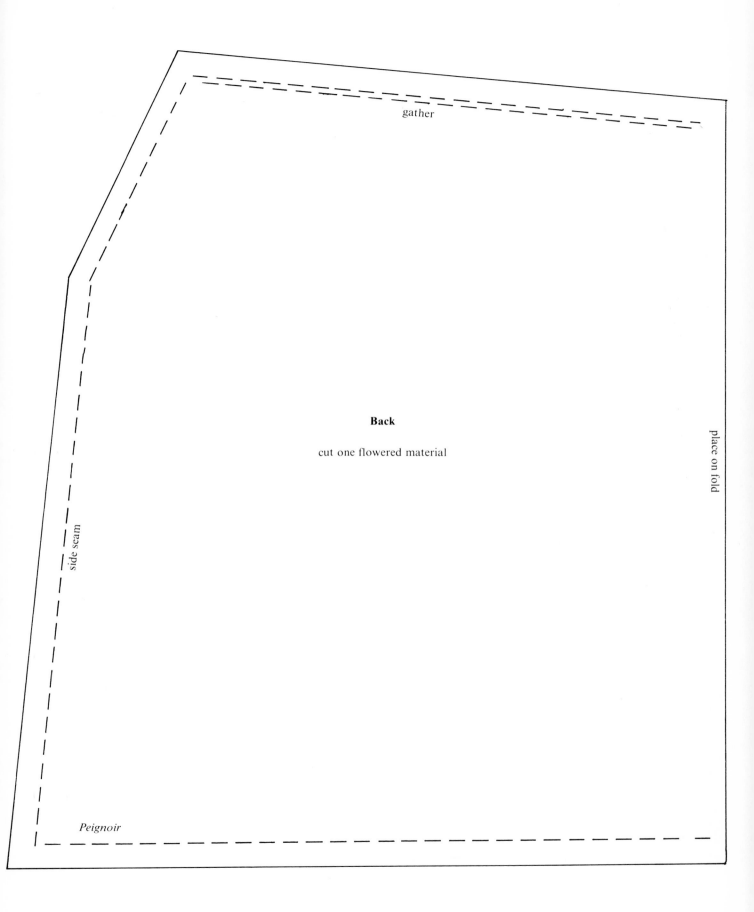

gather

place on fold

Back

cut one flowered material

side seam

Peignoir

Pajamas

Materials:
1/4yd (.23m) lightweight flowered satin
2yd (1.82m) of 1/2in (1.3cm) Gemini
  rayon ribbon
2yd (1.82m) of 1/2in (1.3cm) wide net
Neckband: 6in (15.2cm) long, 1in (2cm)
  wide

Be sure to measure garment on doll as you sew.

See suggestions at end of instructions before purchasing fabric.

TOP: With right sides facing, lay fronts on back and sew shoulder and sleeve seams to within 1in (2cm) from bottom of sleeve. Press seams open and hem bottom of sleeves and vents as shown on pattern. Now sew underarm and side seams to within 1¾in (4cm) from bottom of piece. Clip seams at underarm and press seams open, hem bottom and vents in same manner as sleeves.

FRONT HEMS: Fold back 3/8in (.9cm) (from wrong side to right side), and sew across top. Turn to right side and sew hem on each side on fronts.

NECKBAND: Hold wrong side of neckband towards you and turn 1/4in (.65cm) hem at end on wrong side.

Now lay right side of band on right side of neck edge and sew around piece (3/8in [.9cm] from front hem on both ends). Now turn band under 1/4in (.65cm) and sew on right side but do not allow stitching to show on band. Press lightly on wrong side.

PANTS: With right sides facing, cut two fronts and two backs. Sew center seam together on fronts. Now sew vents on each side of backs from notch to top. With right sides towards you, lay back pieces separate with vents facing. Now lay right side of fronts on backs (right sides will be facing), and sew side seams to within 1½in (3.8cm) of bottom. Press seams open and sew seam on each side of opening on both legs. Hem bottoms. With right sides facing, sew backs together from notch to crotch. Hem top of pants. Baste seams open and press. Turn to right side and press crease in pants lightly on right side.

ROSEBUDS: [Directions for net are in brackets.] Fold 1/2in (1.3cm) Gemini ribbon [net] in half and, starting at the end of the piece, fold 1/2in (1.3cm) towards you on wrong side. Now roll folded edge of ribbon three times [net,

five times] forming a tube. Sew bottom of tube firmly. Now hold ribbon [net] toward you and make a complete diagonal fold. Hold tube firmly between thumb and finger and stitch bottom of tube. Make another fold in same manner [net, one more fold] from right hand to left, around tube. Fold end toward piece and fold to end of bottom of tube, stitch in place and cut end, fasten to bottom. As you make each rosebud or cluster at the front of the pajamas, sew on snaps at the same time. Sew two rosebuds at each opening of the top and the pants.

SUGGESTIONS: Gemini is a very lightweight ribbon, sold in knitting shops, used for the rosebuds on the pajamas. Satin ribbon is too heavy for these tiny rosebuds. You can make the rosebuds a little larger if desired and only use one or two on the front of the pajamas. The rosebuds on the slips (see directions for slips) were made of nylon net. With 2¾in (7cm) of contrasting satin ribbon, fold in half toward center on wrong side and sew together. Now sew three net rosebuds on right side of ribbon. Sew on slip as shown in illustration. □

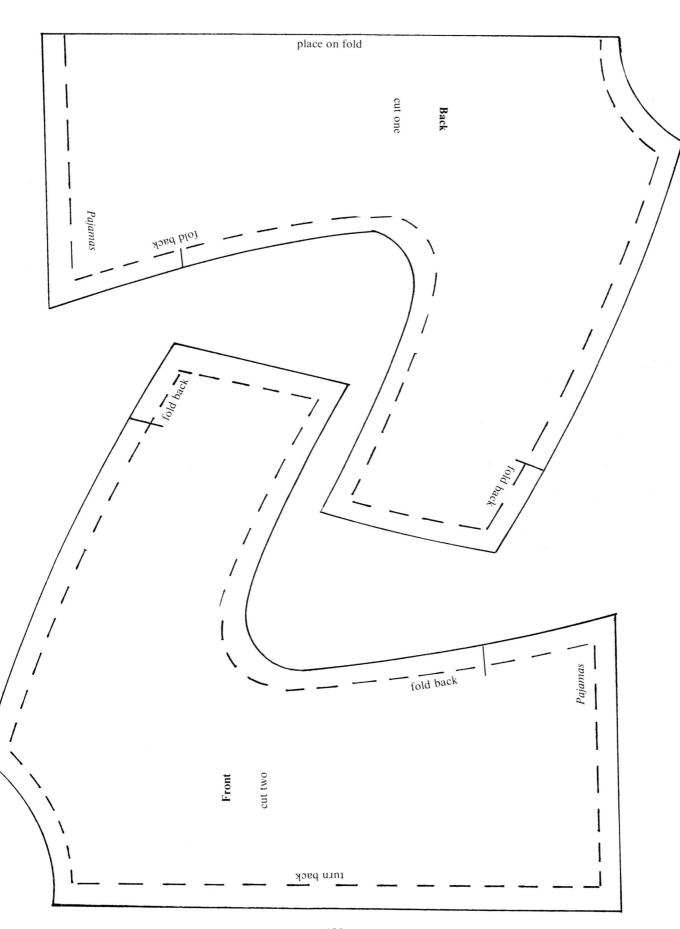

place on fold

Back

cut one

Pajamas

fold back

fold back

fold back

fold back

Pajamas

fold back

Front

cut two

turn back

129

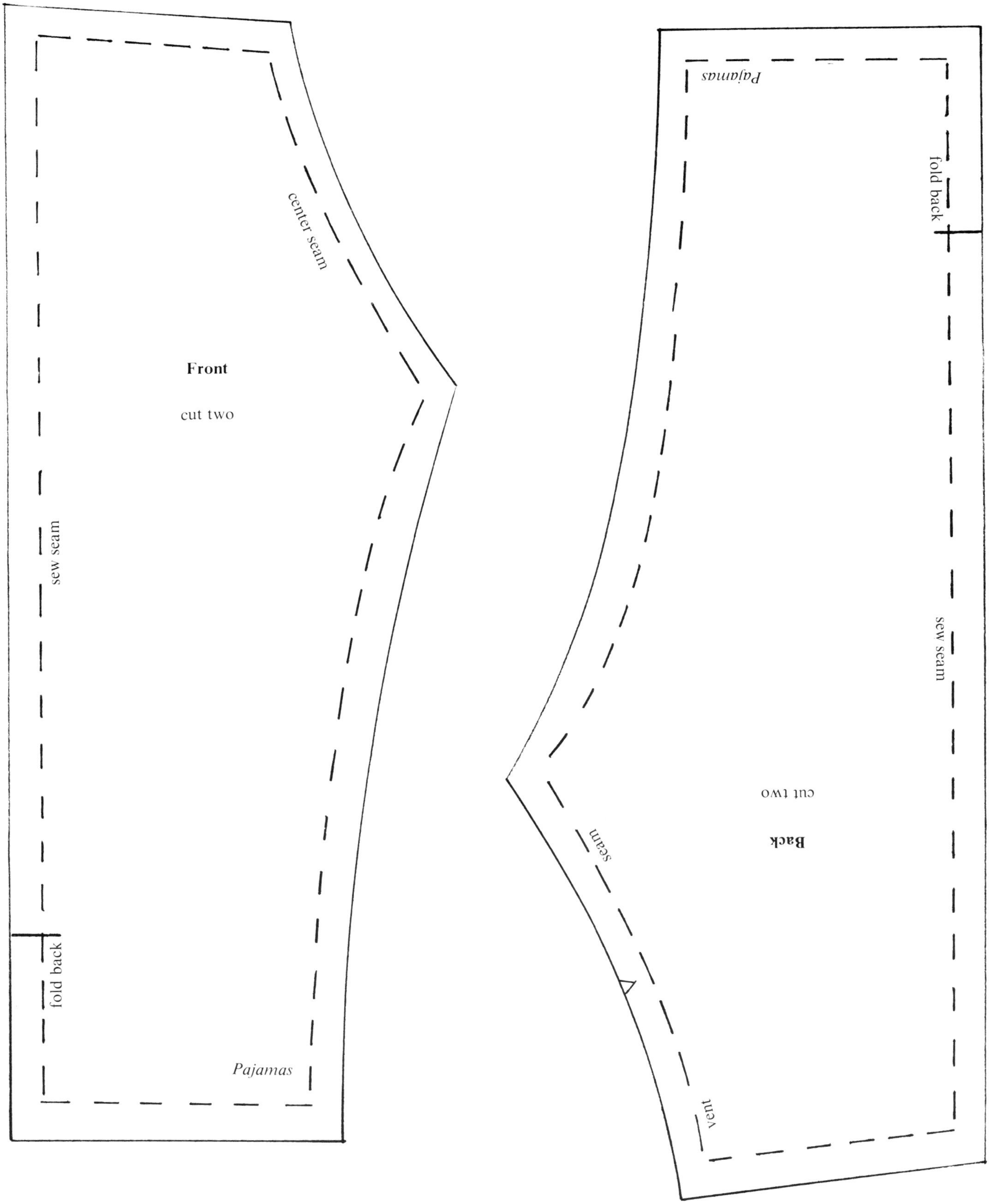

Front

cut two

center seam

sew seam

fold back

Pajamas

Back

cut two

Pajamas

fold back

sew seam

seam

vent

Slips

Materials:

Taffeta or lightweight satin

1¼yd (1.14m) of 1/4in (.65cm) lace

5½in (14cm) of 1/2in (1.3cm) elastic, for Slip A

Waistband for Slip B: 7in (17.8cm) long, 1⅛in (2.8cm) wide

Slip: 5in (12.7cm) long, 28in (71.1cm) wide

Ruffle: 35in (88.9cm) long, 2½in (6.4cm) wide

See suggestions at end of instructions. Be sure to measure garment on doll as you sew.

SLIP A (with elastic band): Mark center of slip, top and bottom. Mark center of ruffle and turn hem under 1/4in (.65cm) and gather lace on right side. Gather ruffle to measure same as bottom of slip. With right sides facing, sew ruffle to bottom of slip, having centers meet. Turn to right side and topstitch. Gather top of slip to measure about 12in (30.5cm). Mark center of elastic and on right side sew elastic over gathers, stretching elastic while you sew. Be sure to have centers meet. With right sides together, sew back of slip.

SLIP B (with fabric band): Hem vents at back, starting 3½in (8.9cm) from bottom. Gather slip to measure 6¼in (15.9cm).

BAND: Mark center of band and turn end of band to wrong side 1/4in (.65cm) at each end. With right sides together, sew band over gathers, having centers meet. Turn band under to wrong side over gathers and sew on right side close to band, but do not allow stitching to show on band. Sew back on slip to vents and sew on snaps.

SUGGESTIONS: Measure gown for which you are making the slip before cutting fabric. The slip should be 1/2in (1.3cm) shorter than the gown and 1in (2.5cm) less in width. See suggestions for rosebuds at the end of the instructions for the Pajamas.

NOTE: Instructions for long, short and circular slips are found with the patterns for the costumes for Cinderella, Fairy Godmother, Bo-Peep, Snow White, Fairy Princess, Mars, Saturn, Uranus and Neptune. □

Panties

Materials:

1/3yd (.30m) taffeta or lightweight fabric

16in (40.6cm) of 1/4in (.65cm) wide lace

4¾in (12.2cm) of 1/8in (.31cm) wide elastic

4¼in (10.9cm) of narrow satin ribbon

PANTIES A: Hem legs of panties on each side. Now gather lace on right side of hem on both leg openings. With right sides facing, sew one side of piece. Mark center of elastic and lay elastic on wrong side below edge. Turn hem over elastic and sew on wrong side, stretching elastic while sewing. Be sure center of elastic meets side seam. Sew other side of panties. Sew tiny bow on pantie leg.

PANTIES B: With right sides facing, sew fronts together from top to crotch.

Hem vents at back and sew across top. Clip seams at front. Hem legs and gather on lace. Sew backs together from notch to crotch. With right sides together, fold in half so centers meet. Sew crotch. Sew on snaps.

NOTE: Instructions for panties are also to be found with the patterns for the costumes for Mercury and Heidi and instructions for pantaloons are found with the patterns for the costume for Miss Muffet.

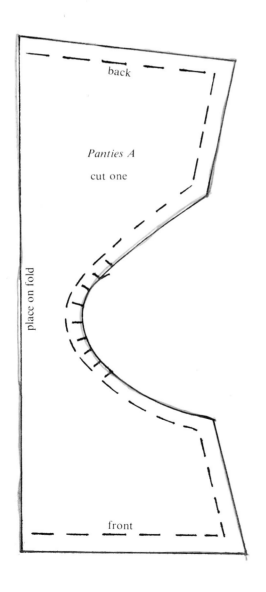

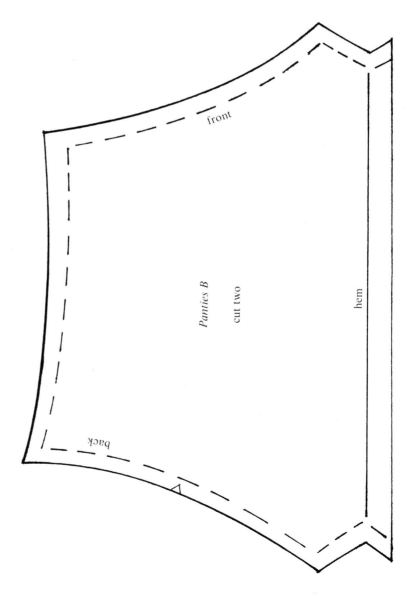

132

Stockings

Materials:
7in (17.8cm) of 7in (17.8cm) wide sheer
stretch material, nylon stretch
material

STOCKINGS: The same pattern can
be used with all of the above-mentioned
fabrics. Do not make a hem on the
spandex fabric as it is a heavier weight
than nylon. Cut two pieces as shown
on the pattern. Turn top of piece for
hem 1/2in (1.3cm) on wrong side. Sew
top of hem at seam with a few stitches
by hand. Now sew seam together,
stretching slightly while sewing; turn to
right side. The white hose is made of
spandex.
NOTE: Instructions for stockings are
also to be found with the patterns for
the costumes for Alice in Wonderland,
Hansel and Gretel.

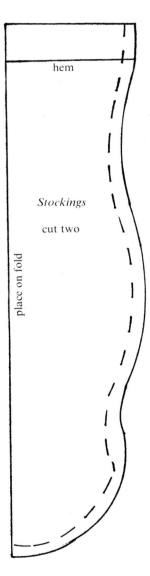

Shoes and Mules

Materials (for shoes):

8in (20.3cm) of 4in (10.2cm) wide leather or suede

4in (10.2cm) of 6in (15.2cm) wide and 1/16in (.15cm) deep cardboard for the soles and heels

Elmer's glue

4in (10.2cm) of 4in (10.2cm) wide iron-on backing for lightweight fabrics

Measure shoes on the doll as you work. If you are using fabric other than leather, suede or fabric of similar weight, see suggestions at the end of instructions.

SHOES A: With cardboard, cut four soles and two heels. Now cut two pieces of leather or fabric of similar weight from pattern. On top and bottom edge of shoe, cut perpendicular to the raw edge, 1/8in (.31cm) deep as shown on pattern. Utilizing a toothpick, dab glue on wrong side of shoe on each side of center, at top of shoes, about 1/8in (.31cm) deep. Allow glue to absorb a minute or two before

turning down; hold firmly until securely fastened. Continue around shoe in same manner. Baste backs; holding wrong sides together, insert foot through opening to insure proper size. Shoe should fit rather tightly in suede and leather as they have a tendency to stretch. Adjust if necessary and sew by machine, with right sides together. Now open seam edges and glue to back of shoe. Turn to right side.

SOLE: Mark center front of sole and insert into wrong side of shoe. Now glue to sections at front of shoe and turn over sole. Hold firmly until fastened, same as top of shoe. Work two sections at a time, starting at back and continuing on each side of sole until bottom of shoe is securely fastened. When thoroughly dry, glue over edges on sole. Now glue entirely over wrong side of second sole. When glue is sufficiently absorbed, place over shoe and hold firmly until completely dry. Glue heel in same manner.

SHOE B: See materials and directions for Shoe A. Work in same manner as Shoe A except at top of edge of shoe, machine-stitch as shown on pattern.

The shoe, when finished, will be about the same size.

Materials (for mules):

Suede, or fabric to match garment, and leather

Elmer's glue

4in (10.2cm) of 6in (15.2cm) wide and 1/16in (.15cm) deep cardboard for the soles and heels

4in (10.2cm) of 4in (10.2cm) wide iron-on backing for lightweight fabrics

2¾in (7.1cm) of 7/8in (2.2cm) wide binding

Measure mules on the doll as you work.

See suggestions at the end of instructions.

MULES: Cut four soles and two heels from cardboard, as shown on pattern. If fabric is lightweight and not leather, use iron-on backing before cutting pattern. Place rough side of backing on wrong side of fabric and press with steam iron. Now cut two pieces for mules as shown on pattern. Cut bias piece but do not use backing. With

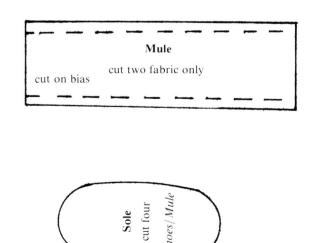

Mule

cut two fabric only

cut on bias

Sole

cut four

Shoes/Mule

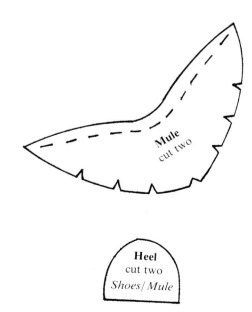

Mule

cut two

Heel

cut two

Shoes/Mule

right sides facing, lay binding on top edge of mule and sew across top. Turn binding over raw edge and sew on right side. Stitch close to binding. Trim ends and back of binding. Cut wedges on bottom, as shown on pattern. Be careful not to cut wedges too wide or too deep. These can be adjusted as you work.

SOLE: Now hold inside of sole towards you and mark center front. Lay wrong side of fabric under sole, having centers meet. Utilizing a toothpick, glue two sections at center front and tip of sole about 1/8in (.31cm) deep. Wait a minute or two until glue is partly absorbed. Then fold fabric over sole and hold until firmly fastened. Continue gluing, working on inside of sole, two sections at a time, until one side is completed. Place mule on foot of doll and turn side under to insure proper fit. Now glue in same manner as other side. When completely fastened and dry, glue over fabric and sole. Glue lightly over second sole; when partly absorbed, place over bottom of shoe. Glue on heel in same manner.

SUGGESTIONS: Be sure leather and suede shoes fit tightly as leather and suede stretch more than fabric with backing. When finished, if shoe seems to fit too tight, use a small pair of scissors and partly open to use as a shoe horn and the shoe will slide right over the heel. There are different weights for backing. If your fabric is rather heavy, use a lighter weight backing, and if lightweight, use a heavier backing. The same sole and heel is used for the shoes and the mules. □

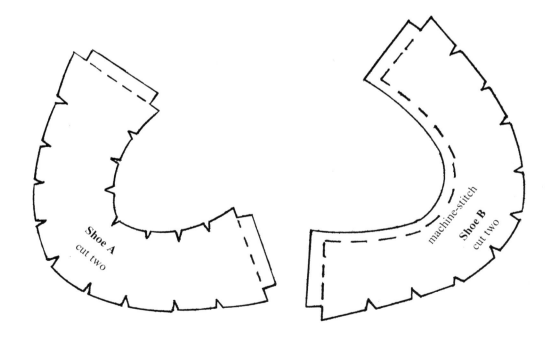

Shoe A cut two

machine-stitch Shoe B cut two